THE TRAGEDIE OF OTHELLO, THE MOORE OF VENICE

By William Shakespeare

Actus Primus. Scoena Prima.

Enter Rodorigo, and Iago.

  Rodorigo. Neuer tell me, I take it much vnkindly
That thou (Iago) who hast had my purse,
As if y strings were thine, should'st know of this

  Ia. But you'l not heare me. If euer I did dream
Of such a matter, abhorre me

  Rodo. Thou told'st me,
Thou did'st hold him in thy hate

  Iago. Despise me
If I do not. Three Great-ones of the Cittie,
(In personall suite to make me his Lieutenant)
Off-capt to him: and by the faith of man
I know my price, I am worth no worsse a place.
But he (as louing his owne pride, and purposes)
Euades them, with a bumbast Circumstance,
Horribly stufft with Epithites of warre,
Non-suites my Mediators. For certes, saies he,
I haue already chose my Officer. And what was he?
For-sooth, a great Arithmatician,
One Michaell Cassio, a Florentine,
(A Fellow almost damn'd in a faire Wife)
That neuer set a Squadron in the Field,
Nor the deuision of a Battaile knowes
More then a Spinster. Vnlesse the Bookish Theoricke:
Wherein the Tongued Consuls can propose
As Masterly as he. Meere pratle (without practise)
Is all his Souldiership. But he (Sir) had th' election;
And I (of whom his eies had seene the proofe
At Rhodes, at Ciprus, and on others grounds
Christen'd, and Heathen) must be be-leed, and calm'd
By Debitor, and Creditor. This Counter-caster,
He (in good time) must his Lieutenant be,
And I (blesse the marke) his Mooreships Auntient

Rod. By heauen, I rather would haue bin his hangman

Iago. Why, there's no remedie.
'Tis the cursse of Seruice;
Preferment goes by Letter, and affection,
And not by old gradation, where each second
Stood Heire to'th' first. Now Sir, be iudge your selfe,
Whether I in any iust terme am Affin'd
To loue the Moore?
Rod. I would not follow him then

Iago. O Sir content you.
I follow him, to serue my turne vpon him.
We cannot all be Masters, nor all Masters
Cannot be truely follow'd. You shall marke
Many a dutious and knee-crooking knaue;
That (doting on his owne obsequious bondage)
Weares out his time, much like his Masters Asse,
For naught but Prouender, & when he's old Casheer'd.
Whip me such honest knaues. Others there are
Who trym'd in Formes, and visages of Dutie,
Keepe yet their hearts attending on themselues,
And throwing but showes of Seruice on their Lords
Doe well thriue by them.
And when they haue lin'd their Coates
Doe themselues Homage.
These Fellowes haue some soule,
And such a one do I professe my selfe. For (Sir)
It is as sure as you are Rodorigo,
Were I the Moore, I would not be Iago:
In following him, I follow but my selfe.
Heauen is my Iudge, not I for loue and dutie,
But seeming so, for my peculiar end:
For when my outward Action doth demonstrate
The natiue act, and figure of my heart
In Complement externe, 'tis not long after
But I will weare my heart vpon my sleeue
For Dawes to pecke at; I am not what I am

Rod. What a fall Fortune do's the Thicks-lips owe
If he can carry't thus?

Iago. Call vp her Father:
Rowse him, make after him, poyson his delight,
Proclaime him in the Streets. Incense her kinsmen,
And though he in a fertile Clymate dwell,
Plague him with Flies: though that his Ioy be Ioy,
Yet throw such chances of vexation on't,
As it may loose some colour

Rodo. Heere is her Fathers house, Ile call aloud

   Iago. Doe, with like timerous accent, and dire yell,
As when (by Night and Negligence) the Fire
Is spied in populus Citties

Rodo. What hoa: Brabantio, Signior Brabantio, hoa

   Iago. Awake: what hoa, Brabantio: Theeues, Theeues.
Looke to your house, your daughter, and your Bags,
Theeues, Theeues

   Bra. Aboue. What is the reason of this terrible
Summons? What is the matter there?
  Rodo. Signior is all your Familie within?
  Iago. Are your Doores lock'd?
  Bra. Why? Wherefore ask you this?
  Iago. Sir, y'are rob'd, for shame put on your Gowne,
Your heart is burst, you haue lost halfe your soule
Euen now, now, very now, an old blacke Ram
Is tupping your white Ewe. Arise, arise,
Awake the snorting Cittizens with the Bell,
Or else the deuill will make a Grand-sire of you.
Arise I say

   Bra. What, haue you lost your wits?
  Rod. Most reuerend Signior, do you know my voice?
  Bra. Not I: what are you?
  Rod. My name is Rodorigo

   Bra. The worsser welcome:
I haue charg'd thee not to haunt about my doores:
In honest plainenesse thou hast heard me say,
My Daughter is not for thee. And now in madnesse

(Being full of Supper, and distempring draughtes)
Vpon malitious knauerie, dost thou come
To start my quiet

Rod. Sir, Sir, Sir

  Bra. But thou must needs be sure,
My spirits and my place haue in their power
To make this bitter to thee

Rodo. Patience good Sir

  Bra. What tell'st thou me of Robbing?
This is Venice: my house is not a Grange

  Rodo. Most graue Brabantio,
In simple and pure soule, I come to you

Ia. Sir: you are one of those that will not serue God, if the deuill bid you.
Because we come to do you seruice, and you thinke we are Ruffians, you'le
haue your Daughter couer'd with a Barbary horse, you'le haue your
Nephewes neigh to you, you'le haue Coursers for Cozens: and Gennets for
Germaines

  Bra. What prophane wretch art thou?
  Ia. I am one Sir, that comes to tell you, your Daughter
and the Moore, are making the Beast with two backs

Bra. Thou art a Villaine

Iago. You are a Senator

Bra. This thou shalt answere. I know thee Rodorigo

  Rod. Sir, I will answere any thing. But I beseech you
If't be your pleasure, and most wise consent,
(As partly I find it is) that your faire Daughter,
At this odde Euen and dull watch o'th' night
Transported with no worse nor better guard,
But with a knaue of common hire, a Gundelier,
To the grosse claspes of a Lasciuious Moore:
If this be knowne to you, and your Allowance,

We then haue done you bold, and saucie wrongs.
But if you know not this, my Manners tell me,
We haue your wrong rebuke. Do not beleeue
That from the sence of all Ciuilitie,
I thus would play and trifle with your Reuerence.
Your Daughter (if you haue not giuen her leaue)
I say againe, hath made a grosse reuolt,
Tying her Dutie, Beautie, Wit, and Fortunes
In an extrauagant, and wheeling Stranger,
Of here, and euery where: straight satisfie your selfe.
If she be in her Chamber, or your house,
Let loose on me the Iustice of the State
For thus deluding you

  Bra. Strike on the Tinder, hoa:
Giue me a Taper: call vp all my people,
This Accident is not vnlike my dreame,
Beleefe of it oppresses me alreadie.
Light, I say, light.
Enter.

  Iag. Farewell: for I must leaue you.
It seemes not meete, nor wholesome to my place
To be producted, (as if I stay, I shall,)
Against the Moore. For I do know the State,
(How euer this may gall him with some checke)
Cannot with safetie cast-him. For he's embark'd
With such loud reason to the Cyprus Warres,
(Which euen now stands in Act) that for their soules
Another of his Fadome, they haue none,
To lead their Businesse. In which regard,
Though I do hate him as I do hell paines,
Yet, for necessitie of present life,
I must show out a Flag, and signe of Loue,
(Which is indeed but signe) that you shal surely find him
Lead to the Sagitary the raised Search:
And there will I be with him. So farewell.

Enter.

Enter Brabantio, with Seruants and Torches.

Bra. It is too true an euill. Gone she is,
And what's to come of my despised time,
Is naught but bitternesse. Now Rodorigo,
Where didst thou see her? (Oh vnhappie Girle)
With the Moore saist thou? (Who would be a Father?)
How didst thou know 'twas she? (Oh she deceaues me
Past thought:) what said she to you? Get moe Tapers.
Raise all my Kindred. Are they married thinke you?
  Rodo. Truely I thinke they are

  Bra. Oh Heauen: how got she out?
Oh treason of the blood.
Fathers, from hence trust not your Daughters minds
By what you see them act. Is there not Charmes,
By which the propertie of Youth, and Maidhood
May be abus'd? Haue you not read Rodorigo,
Of some such thing?
  Rod. Yes Sir: I haue indeed

  Bra. Call vp my Brother: oh would you had had her.
Some one way, some another. Doe you know
Where we may apprehend her, and the Moore?
  Rod. I thinke I can discouer him, if you please
To get good Guard, and go along with me

  Bra. Pray you lead on. At euery house Ile call,
(I may command at most) get Weapons (hoa)
And raise some speciall Officers of might:
On good Rodorigo, I will deserue your paines.

Exeunt.

Scena Secunda.

Enter Othello, Iago, Attendants, with Torches.

  Ia. Though in the trade of Warre I haue slaine men,
Yet do I hold it very stuffe o'th' conscience
To do no contriu'd Murder: I lacke Iniquitie
Sometime to do me seruice. Nine, or ten times
I had thought t'haue yerk'd him here vnder the Ribbes

Othello. 'Tis better as it is

Iago. Nay but he prated,
And spoke such scuruy, and prouoking termes
Against your Honor, that with the little godlinesse I haue
I did full hard forbeare him. But I pray you Sir,
Are you fast married? Be assur'd of this,
That the Magnifico is much belou'd,
And hath in his effect a voice potentiall
As double as the Dukes: He will diuorce you.
Or put vpon you, what restraint or greeuance,
The Law (with all his might, to enforce it on)
Will giue him Cable

Othel. Let him do his spight;
My Seruices, which I haue done the Signorie
Shall out-tongue his Complaints. 'Tis yet to know,
Which when I know, that boasting is an Honour,
I shall promulgate. I fetch my life and being,
From Men of Royall Seige. And my demerites
May speake (vnbonnetted) to as proud a Fortune
As this that I haue reach'd. For know Iago,
But that I loue the gentle Desdemona,
I would not my vnhoused free condition
Put into Circumscription, and Confine,
For the Seas worth. But looke, what Lights come yond?

Enter Cassio, with Torches.

Iago. Those are the raised Father, and his Friends:
You were best go in

Othel. Not I: I must be found.
My Parts, my Title, and my perfect Soule
Shall manifest me rightly. Is it they?
Iago. By Ianus, I thinke no

Othel. The Seruants of the Dukes?
And my Lieutenant?
The goodnesse of the Night vpon you (Friends)
What is the Newes?

Cassio. The Duke do's greet you (Generall)
And he requires your haste, Post-haste appearance,
Euen on the instant

Othello. What is the matter, thinke you?
Cassio. Something from Cyprus, as I may diuine:
It is a businesse of some heate. The Gallies
Haue sent a dozen sequent Messengers
This very night, at one anothers heeles:
And many of the Consuls, rais'd and met,
Are at the Dukes already. You haue bin hotly call'd for,
When being not at your Lodging to be found,
The Senate hath sent about three seuerall Quests,
To search you out

Othel. 'Tis well I am found by you:
I will but spend a word here in the house,
And goe with you

Cassio. Aunciant, what makes he heere?
Iago. Faith, he to night hath boarded a Land Carract,
If it proue lawfull prize, he's made for euer

Cassio. I do not vnderstand

Iago. He's married

Cassio. To who?
Iago. Marry to- Come Captaine, will you go?
Othel. Haue with you

Cassio. Here comes another Troope to seeke for you.

Enter Brabantio, Rodorigo, with Officers, and Torches.

Iago. It is Brabantio: Generall be aduis'd,
He comes to bad intent

Othello. Holla, stand there

Rodo. Signior, it is the Moore

Bra. Downe with him, Theefe

Iago. You, Rodorigo? Come Sir, I am for you

Othe. Keepe vp your bright Swords, for the dew will rust them. Good
Signior, you shall more command with yeares, then with your Weapons

  Bra. Oh thou foule Theefe,
Where hast thou stow'd my Daughter?
Damn'd as thou art, thou hast enchaunted her
For Ile referre me to all things of sense,
(If she in Chaines of Magick were not bound)
Whether a Maid, so tender, Faire, and Happie,
So opposite to Marriage, that she shun'd
The wealthy curled Deareling of our Nation,
Would euer haue (t' encurre a generall mocke)
Run from her Guardage to the sootie bosome,
Of such a thing as thou: to feare, not to delight?
Iudge me the world, if 'tis not grosse in sense,
That thou hast practis'd on her with foule Charmes,
Abus'd her delicate Youth, with Drugs or Minerals,
That weakens Motion. Ile haue't disputed on,
'Tis probable, and palpable to thinking;
I therefore apprehend and do attach thee,
For an abuser of the World, a practiser
Of Arts inhibited, and out of warrant;
Lay hold vpon him, if he do resist
Subdue him, at his perill

  Othe. Hold your hands
Both you of my inclining, and the rest.
Were it my Cue to fight, I should haue knowne it
Without a Prompter. Whether will you that I goe
To answere this your charge?
  Bra. To Prison, till fit time
Of Law, and course of direct Session
Call thee to answer

  Othe. What if I do obey?
How may the Duke be therewith satisfi'd,
Whose Messengers are heere about my side,
Vpon some present businesse of the State,
To bring me to him

Officer. 'Tis true most worthy Signior,
The Dukes in Counsell, and your Noble selfe,
I am sure is sent for

Bra. How? The Duke in Counsell?
In this time of the night? Bring him away;
Mine's not an idle Cause. The Duke himselfe,
Or any of my Brothers of the State,
Cannot but feele this wrong, as 'twere their owne:
For if such Actions may haue passage free,
Bond-slaues, and Pagans shall our Statesmen be.

Exeunt.

Scaena Tertia.

Enter Duke, Senators, and Officers.

Duke. There's no composition in this Newes,
That giues them Credite

1.Sen. Indeed, they are disproportioned;
My Letters say, a Hundred and seuen Gallies

Duke. And mine a Hundred fortie

2.Sena. And mine two Hundred:
But though they iumpe not on a iust accompt,
(As in these Cases where the ayme reports,
'Tis oft with difference) yet do they all confirme
A Turkish Fleete, and bearing vp to Cyprus

Duke. Nay, it is possible enough to iudgement:
I do not so secure me in the Error,
But the maine Article I do approue
In fearefull sense

Saylor within. What hoa, what hoa, what hoa.

Enter Saylor.

Officer. A Messenger from the Gallies

Duke. Now? What's the businesse?
Sailor. The Turkish Preparation makes for Rhodes,
So was I bid report here to the State,
By Signior Angelo

Duke. How say you by this change?
1.Sen. This cannot be
By no assay of reason. 'Tis a Pageant
To keepe vs in false gaze, when we consider
Th' importancie of Cyprus to the Turke;
And let our selues againe but vnderstand,
That as it more concernes the Turke then Rhodes,
So may he with more facile question beare it,
For that it stands not in such Warrelike brace,
But altogether lackes th' abilities
That Rhodes is dress'd in. If we make thought of this,
We must not thinke the Turke is so vnskillfull,
To leaue that latest, which concernes him first,
Neglecting an attempt of ease, and gaine
To wake, and wage a danger profitlesse

Duke. Nay, in all confidence he's not for Rhodes

Officer. Here is more Newes.

Enter a Messenger.

Messen. The Ottamites, Reueren'd, and Gracious,
Steering with due course toward the Ile of Rhodes,
Haue there inioynted them with an after Fleete

1.Sen. I, so I thought: how many, as you guesse?
Mess. Of thirtie Saile: and now they do re-stem
Their backward course, bearing with frank appearance
Their purposes toward Cyprus. Signior Montano,
Your trustie and most Valiant Seruitour,
With his free dutie, recommends you thus,
And prayes you to beleeue him

Duke. 'Tis certaine then for Cyprus:
Marcus Luccicos is not he in Towne?
1.Sen. He's now in Florence

Duke. Write from vs,
To him, Post, Post-haste, dispatch

1.Sen. Here comes Brabantio, and the Valiant Moore.

Enter Brabantio, Othello, Cassio, Iago, Rodorigo, and Officers.

Duke. Valiant Othello, we must straight employ you,
Against the generall Enemy Ottoman.
I did not see you: welcome gentle Signior,
We lack't your Counsaile, and your helpe to night

Bra. So did I yours: Good your Grace pardon me.
Neither my place, nor ought I heard of businesse
Hath rais'd me from my bed; nor doth the generall care
Take hold on me. For my perticular griefe
Is of so flood-gate, and ore-bearing Nature,
That it engluts, and swallowes other sorrowes,
And it is still it selfe

Duke. Why? What's the matter?
Bra. My Daughter: oh my Daughter!
Sen. Dead?
Bra. I, to me.
She is abus'd, stolne from me, and corrupted
By Spels, and Medicines, bought of Mountebanks;
For Nature, so prepostrously to erre,
(Being not deficient, blind, or lame of sense,)
Sans witch-craft could not

Duke. Who ere he be, that in this foule proceeding
Hath thus beguil'd your Daughter of her selfe,
And you of her; the bloodie Booke of Law,
You shall your selfe read, in the bitter letter,
After your owne sense: yea, though our proper Son
Stood in your Action

Bra. Humbly I thanke your Grace,
Here is the man; this Moore, whom now it seemes
Your speciall Mandate, for the State affaires
Hath hither brought

All. We are verie sorry for't

  Duke. What in your owne part, can you say to this?
  Bra. Nothing, but this is so

  Othe. Most Potent, Graue, and Reueren'd Signiors,
My very Noble, and approu'd good Masters;
That I haue tane away this old mans Daughter,
It is most true: true I haue married her;
The verie head, and front of my offending,
Hath this extent; no more. Rude am I, in my speech,
And little bless'd with the soft phrase of Peace;
For since these Armes of mine, had seuen yeares pith,
Till now, some nine Moones wasted, they haue vs'd
Their deerest action, in the Tented Field:
And little of this great world can I speake,
More then pertaines to Feats of Broiles, and Battaile,
And therefore little shall I grace my cause,
In speaking for my selfe. Yet, (by your gratious patience)
I will a round vn-varnish'd Tale deliuer,
Of my whole course of Loue.
What Drugges, what Charmes,
What Coniuration, and what mighty Magicke,
(For such proceeding I am charg'd withall)
I won his Daughter

  Bra. A Maiden, neuer bold:
Of Spirit so still, and quiet, that her Motion
Blush'd at her selfe, and she, in spight of Nature,
Of Yeares, of Country, Credite, euery thing
To fall in Loue, with what she fear'd to looke on;
It is a iudgement main'd, and most imperfect.
That will confesse Perfection so could erre
Against all rules of Nature, and must be driuen
To find out practises of cunning hell
Why this should be. I therefore vouch againe,
That with some Mixtures, powrefull o're the blood,
Or with some Dram, (coniur'd to this effect)
He wrought vpon her.
To vouch this, is no proofe,
Without more wider, and more ouer Test

Then these thin habits, and poore likely-hoods
Of moderne seeming, do prefer against him

   Sen. But Othello, speake,
Did you, by indirect, and forced courses
Subdue, and poyson this yong Maides affections?
Or came it by request, and such faire question
As soule, to soule affordeth?
  Othel. I do beseech you,
Send for the Lady to the Sagitary,
And let her speake of me before her Father;
If you do finde me foule, in her report,
The Trust, the Office, I do hold of you,
Not onely take away, but let your Sentence
Euen fall vpon my life

Duke. Fetch Desdemona hither

  Othe. Aunciant, conduct them:
You best know the place.
And tell she come, as truely as to heauen,
I do confesse the vices of my blood,
So iustly to your Graue eares, Ile present
How I did thriue in this faire Ladies loue,
And she in mine

Duke. Say it Othello

  Othe. Her Father lou'd me, oft inuited me:
Still question'd me the Storie of my life,
From yeare to yeare: the Battaile, Sieges, Fortune,
That I haue past.
I ran it through, euen from my boyish daies,
Toth' very moment that he bad me tell it.
Wherein I spoke of most disastrous chances:
Of mouing Accidents by Flood and Field,
Of haire-breadth scapes i'th' imminent deadly breach;
Of being taken by the Insolent Foe,
And sold to slauery. Of my redemption thence,
And portance in my Trauellours historie.
Wherein of Antars vast, and Desarts idle,

Rough Quarries, Rocks, Hills, whose head touch heauen,
It was my hint to speake. Such was my Processe,
And of the Canibals that each others eate,
The Antropophague, and men whose heads
Grew beneath their shoulders. These things to heare,
Would Desdemona seriously incline:
But still the house Affaires would draw her hence:
Which euer as she could with haste dispatch,
She'l'd come againe, and with a greedie eare
Deuoure vp my discourse. Which I obseruing,
Tooke once a pliant houre, and found good meanes
To draw from her a prayer of earnest heart,
That I would all my Pilgrimage dilate,
Whereof by parcels she had something heard,
But not instinctiuely: I did consent,
And often did beguile her of her teares,
When I did speake of some distressefull stroke
That my youth suffer'd: My Storie being done,
She gaue me for my paines a world of kisses:
She swore in faith 'twas strange: 'twas passing strange,
'Twas pittifull: 'twas wondrous pittifull.
She wish'd she had not heard it, yet she wish'd
That Heauen had made her such a man. She thank'd me,
And bad me, if I had a Friend that lou'd her,
I should but teach him how to tell my Story,
And that would wooe her. Vpon this hint I spake,
She lou'd me for the dangers I had past,
And I lou'd her, that she did pitty them.
This onely is the witch-craft I haue vs'd.
Here comes the Ladie: Let her witnesse it.

Enter Desdemona, Iago, Attendants.

  Duke. I thinke this tale would win my Daughter too,
Good Brabantio, take vp this mangled matter at the best:
Men do their broken Weapons rather vse,
Then their bare hands

  Bra. I pray you heare her speake?
If she confesse that she was halfe the wooer,
Destruction on my head, if my bad blame

Light on the man. Come hither gentle Mistris,
Do you perceiue in all this Noble Companie,
Where most you owe obedience?
  Des. My Noble Father,
I do perceiue heere a diuided dutie.
To you I am bound for life, and education:
My life and education both do learne me,
How to respect you. You are the Lord of duty,
I am hitherto your Daughter. But heere's my Husband;
And so much dutie, as my Mother shew'd
To you, preferring you before her Father:
So much I challenge, that I may professe
Due to the Moore my Lord

  Bra. God be with you: I haue done.
Please it your Grace, on to the State Affaires;
I had rather to adopt a Child, then get it.
Come hither Moore;
I here do giue thee that with all my heart,
Which but thou hast already, with all my heart
I would keepe from thee. For your sake (Iewell)
I am glad at soule, I haue no other Child,
For thy escape would teach me Tirranie
To hang clogges on them. I haue done my Lord

  Duke. Let me speake like your selfe:
And lay a Sentence,
Which as a grise, or step may helpe these Louers.
When remedies are past, the griefes are ended
By seeing the worst, which late on hopes depended.
To mourne a Mischeefe that is past and gon,
Is the next way to draw new mischiefe on.
What cannot be preseru'd, when Fortune takes:
Patience, her Iniury a mock'ry makes.
The rob'd that smiles, steales something from the Thiefe,
He robs himselfe, that spends a bootelesse griefe

  Bra. So let the Turke of Cyprus vs beguile,
We loose it not so long as we can smile:
He beares the Sentence well, that nothing beares,
But the free comfort which from thence he heares.

But he beares both the Sentence, and the sorrow,
That to pay griefe, must of poore Patience borrow.
These Sentences, to Sugar, or to Gall,
Being strong on both sides, are Equiuocall.
But words are words, I neuer yet did heare:
That the bruized heart was pierc'd through the eares.
I humbly beseech you proceed to th' Affaires of State

Duke. The Turke with a most mighty Preparation makes for Cyprus:
Othello, the Fortitude of the place is best knowne to you. And though we
haue there a Substitute of most allowed sufficiencie; yet opinion, a more
soueraigne Mistris of Effects, throwes a more safer voice on you: you must
therefore be content to slubber the glosse of your new Fortunes, with this
more stubborne, and boystrous expedition

   Othe. The Tirant Custome, most Graue Senators,
Hath made the flinty and Steele Coach of Warre
My thrice-driuen bed of Downe. I do agnize
A Naturall and prompt Alacratie,
I finde in hardnesse: and do vndertake
This present Warres against the Ottamites.
Most humbly therefore bending to your State,
I craue fit disposition for my Wife,
Due reference of Place, and Exhibition,
With such Accomodation and besort
As leuels with her breeding

   Duke. Why at her Fathers?
   Bra. I will not haue it so

Othe. Nor I

   Des. Nor would I there recide,
To put my Father in impatient thoughts
By being in his eye. Most Gracious Duke,
To my vnfolding, lend your prosperous eare,
And let me finde a Charter in your voice
T' assist my simplenesse

   Duke. What would you Desdemona?
   Des. That I loue the Moore, to liue with him,

My downe-right violence, and storme of Fortunes,
May trumpet to the world. My heart's subdu'd
Euen to the very quality of my Lord;
I saw Othello's visage in his mind,
And to his Honours and his valiant parts,
Did I my soule and Fortunes consecrate.
So that (deere Lords) if I be left behind
A Moth of Peace, and he go to the Warre,
The Rites for why I loue him, are bereft me:
And I a heauie interim shall support
By his deere absence. Let me go with him

  Othe. Let her haue your voice.
Vouch with me Heauen, I therefore beg it not
To please the pallate of my Appetite:
Nor to comply with heat the yong affects
In my defunct, and proper satisfaction.
But to be free, and bounteous to her minde:
And Heauen defend your good soules, that you thinke
I will your serious and great businesse scant
When she is with me. No, when light wing'd Toyes
Of feather'd Cupid, seele with wanton dulnesse
My speculatiue, and offic'd Instrument:
That my Disports corrupt, and taint my businesse:
Let House-wiues make a Skillet of my Helme,
And all indigne, and base aduersities,
Make head against my Estimation

  Duke. Be it as you shall priuately determine,
Either for her stay, or going: th' Affaire cries hast:
And speed must answer it

Sen. You must away to night

Othe. With all my heart

  Duke. At nine i'th' morning, here wee'l meete againe.
Othello, leaue some Officer behind
And he shall our Commission bring to you:
And such things else of qualitie and respect
As doth import you

Othe. So please your Grace, my Ancient,
A man he is of honesty and trust:
To his conueyance I assigne my wife,
With what else needfull, your good Grace shall think
To be sent after me

Duke. Let it be so:
Good night to euery one. And Noble Signior,
If Vertue no delighted Beautie lacke,
Your Son-in-law is farre more Faire then Blacke

Sen. Adieu braue Moore, vse Desdemona well

Bra. Looke to her (Moore) if thou hast eies to see:
She ha's deceiu'd her Father, and may thee.
Enter.

Othe. My life vpon her faith. Honest Iago,
My Desdemona must I leaue to thee:
I prythee let thy wife attend on her,
And bring them after in the best aduantage.
Come Desdemona, I haue but an houre
Of Loue, of wordly matter, and direction
To spend with thee. We must obey the time.
Enter.

Rod. Iago

Iago. What saist thou Noble heart?
Rod. What will I do, think'st thou?
Iago. Why go to bed and sleepe

Rod. I will incontinently drowne my selfe

Iago. If thou do'st, I shall neuer loue thee after. Why thou silly
Gentleman? Rod. It is sillynesse to liue, when to liue is torment: and then
haue we a prescription to dye, when death is our Physition

Iago. Oh villanous: I haue look'd vpon the world for foure times seuen
yeares, and since I could distinguish betwixt a Benefit, and an Iniurie: I
neuer found man that knew how to loue himselfe. Ere I would say, I

would drowne my selfe for the loue of a Gynney Hen, I would change my Humanity with a Baboone

    Rod. What should I do? I confesse it is my shame to be so fond, but it is not in my vertue to amend it

Iago. Vertue? A figge, 'tis in our selues that we are thus, or thus. Our Bodies are our Gardens, to the which, our Wills are Gardiners. So that if we will plant Nettels, or sowe Lettice: Set Hisope, and weede vp Time: Supplie it with one gender of Hearbes, or distract it with many: either to haue it sterrill with idlenesse, or manured with Industry, why the power, and Corrigeable authoritie of this lies in our Wills. If the braine of our liues had not one Scale of Reason, to poize another of Sensualitie, the blood, and basenesse of our Natures would conduct vs to most prepostrous Conclusions. But we haue Reason to coole our raging Motions, our carnall Stings, or vnbitted Lusts: whereof I take this, that you call Loue, to be a Sect, or Seyen

Rod. It cannot be

Iago. It is meerly a Lust of the blood, and a permission of the will. Come, be a man: drowne thy selfe? Drown Cats, and blind Puppies. I haue profest me thy Friend, and I confesse me knit to thy deseruing, with Cables of perdurable toughnesse. I could neuer better steed thee then now. Put Money in thy purse: follow thou the Warres, defeate thy fauour, with an vsurp'd Beard. I say put Money in thy purse. It cannot be long that Desdemona should continue her loue to the Moore. Put Money in thy purse: nor he his to her. It was a violent Commencement in her, and thou shalt see an answerable Sequestration, put but Money in thy purse. These Moores are changeable in their wils: fill thy purse with Money. The Food that to him now is as lushious as Locusts, shalbe to him shortly, as bitter as Coloquintida. She must change for youth: when she is sated with his body she will find the errors of her choice. Therefore, put Money in thy purse. If thou wilt needs damne thy selfe, do it a more delicate way then drowning. Make all the Money thou canst: If Sanctimonie, and a fraile vow, betwixt an erring Barbarian, and super-subtle Venetian be not too hard for my wits, and all the Tribe of hell, thou shalt enioy her: therefore make Money: a pox of drowning thy selfe, it is cleane out of the way. Seeke thou rather to be hang'd in Compassing thy ioy, then to be drown'd, and go without her

Rodo. Wilt thou be fast to my hopes, if I depend on the issue? Iago. Thou art sure of me: Go make Money: I haue told thee often, and I re-tell thee againe, and againe, I hate the Moore. My cause is hearted; thine hath no lesse reason. Let vs be coniunctiue in our reuenge, against him. If thou canst Cuckold him, thou dost thy selfe a pleasure, me a sport. There are many Euents in the Wombe of Time, which wilbe deliuered. Trauerse, go, prouide thy Money. We will haue more of this to morrow. Adieu

  Rod. Where shall we meete i'th' morning?
  Iago. At my Lodging

Rod. Ile be with thee betimes

  Iago. Go too, farewell. Do you heare Rodorigo?
  Rod. Ile sell all my Land.
Enter.

  Iago. Thus do I euer make my Foole, my purse:
For I mine owne gain'd knowledge should prophane
If I would time expend with such Snipe,
But for my Sport, and Profit: I hate the Moore,
And it is thought abroad, that 'twixt my sheets
She ha's done my Office. I know not if't be true,
But I, for meere suspition in that kinde,
Will do, as if for Surety. He holds me well,
The better shall my purpose worke on him:
Cassio's a proper man: Let me see now,
To get his Place, and to plume vp my will
In double Knauery. How? How? Let's see.
After some time, to abuse Othello's eares,
That he is too familiar with his wife:
He hath a person, and a smooth dispose
To be suspected: fram'd to make women false.
The Moore is of a free, and open Nature,
That thinkes men honest, that but seeme to be so,
And will as tenderly be lead by'th' Nose
As Asses are:
I hau't: it is engendred: Hell, and Night,
Must bring this monstrous Birth, to the worlds light.

Actus Secundus. Scena Prima.

Enter Montano, and two Gentlemen.

  Mon. What from the Cape, can you discerne at Sea?
  1.Gent. Nothing at all, it is a high wrought Flood:
I cannot 'twixt the Heauen, and the Maine,
Descry a Saile

  Mon. Me thinks, the wind hath spoke aloud at Land,
A fuller blast ne're shooke our Battlements:
If it hath ruffiand so vpon the Sea,
What ribbes of Oake, when Mountaines melt on them,
Can hold the Morties. What shall we heare of this?
  2 A Segregation of the Turkish Fleet:
For do but stand vpon the Foaming Shore,
The chidden Billow seemes to pelt the Clowds,
The winde-shak'd-Surge, with high & monstrous Maine
Seemes to cast water on the burning Beare,
And quench the Guards of th' euer-fixed Pole:
I neuer did like mollestation view
On the enchafed Flood

  Men. If that the Turkish Fleete
Be not enshelter'd, and embay'd, they are drown'd,
It is impossible to beare it out.
Enter a Gentleman.

  3 Newes Laddes: our warres are done:
The desperate Tempest hath so bang'd the Turkes,
That their designement halts. A Noble ship of Venice,
Hath seene a greeuous wracke and sufferance
On most part of their Fleet

  Mon. How? Is this true?
  3 The Ship is heere put in: A Verennessa, Michael Cassio
Lieutenant to the warlike Moore, Othello,
Is come on Shore: the Moore himselfe at Sea,
And is in full Commission heere for Cyprus

  Mon. I am glad on't:
'Tis a worthy Gouernour

3 But this same Cassio, though he speake of comfort,
Touching the Turkish losse, yet he lookes sadly,
And praye the Moore be safe; for they were parted
With fowle and violent Tempest

   Mon. Pray Heauens he be:
For I haue seru'd him, and the man commands
Like a full Soldier. Let's to the Sea-side (hoa)
As well to see the Vessell that's come in,
As to throw-out our eyes for braue Othello,
Euen till we make the Maine, and th' Eriall blew,
An indistinct regard

   Gent. Come, let's do so;
For euery Minute is expectancie
Of more Arriuancie.
Enter Cassio.

  Cassi. Thankes you, the valiant of the warlike Isle,
That so approoue the Moore: Oh let the Heauens
Giue him defence against the Elements,
For I haue lost him on a dangerous Sea

   Mon. Is he well ship'd?
  Cassio. His Barke is stoutly Timber'd, and his Pylot
Of verie expert, and approu'd Allowance;
Therefore my hope's (not surfetted to death)
Stand in bold Cure

Within. A Saile, a Saile, a Saile

  Cassio. What noise?
  Gent. The Towne is empty; on the brow o'th' Sea
Stand rankes of People and they cry, a Saile

Cassio. My hopes do shape him for the Gouernor

  Gent. They do discharge their Shot of Courtesie,
Our Friends, at least

  Cassio. I pray you Sir, go forth,
And giue vs truth who 'tis that is arriu'd

Gent. I shall.
Enter.

Mon. But good Lieutenant, is your Generall wiu'd?
Cassio. Most fortunately: he hath atchieu'd a Maid
That paragons description, and wilde Fame:
One that excels the quirkes of Blazoning pens,
And in th' essentiall Vesture of Creation,
Do's tyre the Ingeniuer.
Enter Gentleman.

How now? Who ha's put in?
Gent. 'Tis one Iago, Auncient to the Generall

Cassio. Ha's had most fauourable, and happie speed:
Tempests themselues, high Seas, and howling windes,
The gutter'd-Rockes, and Congregated Sands,
Traitors ensteep'd, to enclogge the guiltlesse Keele,
As hauing sence of Beautie, do omit
Their mortall Natures, letting go safely by
The Diuine Desdemona

Mon. What is she?
Cassio. She that I spake of:
Our great Captains Captaine,
Left in the conduct of the bold Iago,
Whose footing heere anticipates our thoughts,
A Senights speed. Great Ioue, Othello guard,
And swell his Saile with thine owne powrefull breath,
That he may blesse this Bay with his tall Ship,
Make loues quicke pants in Desdemonaes Armes,
Giue renew'd fire to our extincted Spirits.

Enter Desdemona, Iago, Rodorigo, and Aemilia.

Oh behold,
The Riches of the Ship is come on shore:
You men of Cyprus, let her haue your knees.
Haile to thee Ladie: and the grace of Heauen,
Before, behinde thee, and on euery hand
Enwheele thee round

Des. I thanke you, Valiant Cassio,
What tydings can you tell of my Lord?
  Cas. He is not yet arriu'd, nor know I ought
But that he's well, and will be shortly heere

  Des. Oh, but I feare:
How lost you company?
  Cassio. The great Contention of Sea, and Skies
Parted our fellowship. But hearke, a Saile

Within. A Saile, a Saile

  Gent. They giue this greeting to the Cittadell:
This likewise is a Friend

  Cassio. See for the Newes:
Good Ancient, you are welcome. Welcome Mistris:
Let it not gaule your patience (good Iago)
That I extend my Manners. 'Tis my breeding,
That giues me this bold shew of Curtesie

  Iago. Sir, would she giue you so much of her lippes,
As of her tongue she oft bestowes on me,
You would haue enough

Des. Alas: she ha's no speech

  Iago. Infaith too much:
I finde it still, when I haue leaue to sleepe.
Marry before your Ladyship, I grant,
She puts her tongue a little in her heart,
And chides with thinking

aemil. You haue little cause to say so

  Iago. Come on, come on: you are Pictures out of
doore: Bells in your Parlours: Wilde-Cats in your Kitchens:
Saints in your Iniuries: Diuels being offended:
Players in your Huswiferie, and Huswiues in your
Beds

Des. Oh, fie vpon thee, Slanderer

Iago. Nay, it is true: or else I am a Turke,
You rise to play, and go to bed to worke.
Aemil. You shall not write my praise

Iago. No, let me not

   Desde. What would'st write of me, if thou should'st
praise me?
   Iago. Oh, gentle Lady, do not put me too't,
For I am nothing, if not Criticall

   Des. Come on, assay.
There's one gone to the Harbour?
   Iago. I Madam

   Des. I am not merry: but I do beguile
The thing I am, by seeming otherwise.
Come, how would'st thou praise me?
   Iago. I am about it, but indeed my inuention comes
from my pate, as Birdlyme do's from Freeze, it pluckes
out Braines and all. But my Muse labours, and thus she
is deliuer'd.
If she be faire, and wise: fairenesse, and wit,
The ones for vse, the other vseth it

   Des. Well prais'd:
How if she be Blacke and Witty?
   Iago. If she be blacke, and thereto haue a wit,
She'le find a white, that shall her blacknesse fit

   Des. Worse, and worse.
Aemil. How if Faire, and Foolish?
   Iago. She neuer yet was foolish that was faire,
For euen her folly helpt her to an heire

Desde. These are old fond Paradoxes, to make Fooles laugh i'th' Alehouse.
What miserable praise hast thou for her that's Foule, and Foolish

   Iago. There's none so foule and foolish thereunto,
But do's foule pranks, which faire, and wise-ones do

Desde. Oh heauy ignorance: thou praisest the worst best. But what praise could'st thou bestow on a deseruing woman indeed? One, that in the authorithy of her merit, did iustly put on the vouch of very malice it selfe

  Iago. She that was euer faire, and neuer proud,
Had Tongue at will, and yet was neuer loud:
Neuer lackt Gold, and yet went neuer gay,
Fled from her wish, and yet said now I may.
She that being angred, her reuenge being nie,
Bad her wrong stay, and her displeasure flie:
She that in wisedome neuer was so fraile,
To change the Cods-head for the Salmons taile:
She that could thinke, and neu'r disclose her mind,
See Suitors following, and not looke behind:
She was a wight, (if euer such wightes were)
  Des. To do what?
  Iago. To suckle Fooles, and chronicle small Beere

Desde. Oh most lame and impotent conclusion. Do not learne of him aemillia, though he be thy husband. How say you (Cassio) is he not a most prophane, and liberall Counsailor? Cassio. He speakes home (Madam) you may rellish him more in the Souldier, then in the Scholler

Iago. He takes her by the palme: I, well said, whisper. With as little a web as this, will I ensnare as great a Fly as Cassio. I smile vpon her, do: I will giue thee in thine owne Courtship. You say true, 'tis so indeed. If such tricks as these strip you out of your Lieutenantrie, it had beene better you had not kiss'd your three fingers so oft, which now againe you are most apt to play the Sir, in. Very good: well kiss'd, and excellent Curtsie: 'tis so indeed. Yet againe, your fingers to your lippes? Would they were Cluster-pipes for your sake. The Moore I know his Trumpet

Cassio. 'Tis truely so

Des. Let's meete him, and recieue him

  Cassio. Loe, where he comes.
Enter Othello, and Attendants.

Oth. O, my faire Warriour

Des. My deere Othello

Othe. It giues me wonder great, as my content
To see you heere before me.
Oh my Soules Ioy:
If after euery Tempest, come such Calmes,
May the windes blow, till they haue waken'd death:
And let the labouring Barke climbe hills of Seas
Olympus high: and duck againe as low,
As hell's from Heauen. If it were now to dye,
'Twere now to be most happy. For I feare,
My Soule hath her content so absolute,
That not another comfort like to this,
Succeedes in vnknowne Fate

Des. The Heauens forbid
But that our Loues
And Comforts should encrease
Euen as our dayes do grow

Othe. Amen to that (sweet Powers)
I cannot speake enough of this content,
It stoppes me heere: it is too much of ioy.
And this, and this the greatest discords be
That ere our hearts shall make

Iago. Oh you are well tun'd now: But Ile set downe
the peggs that make this Musicke, as honest as I am

Othe. Come: let vs to the Castle.
Newes (Friends) our Warres are done:
The Turkes are drown'd.
How do's my old Acquaintance of this Isle?
(Hony) you shall be well desir'd in Cyprus,
I haue found great loue among'st them. Oh my Sweet,
I prattle out of fashion, and I doate
In mine owne comforts. I prythee, good Iago,
Go to the Bay, and disimbarke my Coffers:
Bring thou the Master to the Cittadell,
He is a good one, and his worthynesse
Do's challenge much respect. Come Desdemona,
Once more well met at Cyprus.

Exit Othello and Desdemona.

Iago. Do thou meet me presently at the Harbour. Come thither, if thou be'st Valiant, (as they say base men being in Loue, haue then a Nobilitie in their Natures, more then is natiue to them) list-me; the Lieutenant to night watches on the Court of Guard. First, I must tell thee this: Desdemona, is directly in loue with him

Rod. With him? Why, 'tis not possible

Iago. Lay thy finger thus: and let thy soule be instructed. Marke me with what violence she first lou'd the Moore, but for bragging, and telling her fantasticall lies. To loue him still for prating, let not thy discreet heart thinke it. Her eye must be fed. And what delight shall she haue to looke on the diuell? When the Blood is made dull with the Act of Sport, there should be a game to enflame it, and to giue Satiety a fresh appetite. Louelinesse in fauour, simpathy in yeares, Manners, and Beauties: all which the Moore is defectiue in. Now for want of these requir'd Conueniences, her delicate tendernesse wil finde it selfe abus'd, begin to heaue the, gorge, disrellish and abhorre the Moore, very Nature wil instruct her in it, and compell her to some second choice. Now Sir, this granted (as it is a most pregnant and vnforc'd position) who stands so eminent in the degree of this Fortune, as Cassio do's: a knaue very voluble: no further conscionable, then in putting on the meere forme of Ciuill, and Humaine seeming, for the better compasse of his salt, and most hidden loose Affection? Why none, why none: A slipper, and subtle knaue, a finder of occasion: that he's an eye can stampe, and counterfeit Aduantages, though true Aduantage neuer present it selfe. A diuelish knaue: besides, the knaue is handsome, young: and hath all those requisites in him, that folly and greene mindes looke after. A pestilent compleat knaue, and the woman hath found him already

    Rodo. I cannot beleeue that in her, she's full of most bless'd condition

Iago. Bless'd figges-end. The Wine she drinkes is made of grapes. If shee had beene bless'd, shee would neuer haue lou'd the Moore: Bless'd pudding. Didst thou not see her paddle with the palme of his hand? Didst not marke that? Rod. Yes, that I did: but that was but curtesie

Iago . Leacherie by this hand: an Index, and obscure prologue to the History of Lust and foule Thoughts. They met so neere with their lippes, that their breathes embrac'd together. Villanous thoughts Rodorigo, when these mutabilities so marshall the way, hard at hand comes the Master, and maine exercise, th' incorporate conclusion: Pish. But Sir, be you rul'd by me. I haue brought you from Venice. Watch you to night: for the Command, Ile lay't vpon you. Cassio knowes you not: Ile not be farre from you. Do you finde some occasion to anger Cassio, either by speaking too loud, or tainting his discipline, or from what other course you please, which the time shall more fauorably minister

Rod. Well

Iago. Sir, he's rash, and very sodaine in Choller: and happely may strike at you, prouoke him that he may: for euen out of that will I cause these of Cyprus to Mutiny. Whose qualification shall come into no true taste againe, but by the displanting of Cassio. So shall you haue a shorter iourney to your desires, by the meanes I shall then haue to preferre them. And the impediment most profitably remoued, without the which there were no expectation of our prosperitie

Rodo. I will do this, if you can bring it to any opportunity

   Iago. I warrant thee. Meete me by and by at the
Cittadell. I must fetch his Necessaries a Shore. Farewell

   Rodo. Adieu.
Enter.

   Iago. That Cassio loues her, I do well beleeu't:
That she loues him, 'tis apt, and of great Credite.
The Moore (howbeit that I endure him not)
Is of a constant, louing, Noble Nature,
And I dare thinke, he'le proue to Desdemona
A most deere husband. Now I do loue her too,
Not out of absolute Lust, (though peraduenture
I stand accomptant for as great a sin)
But partely led to dyet my Reuenge,
For that I do suspect the lustie Moore
Hath leap'd into my Seate. The thought whereof,
Doth (like a poysonous Minerall) gnaw my Inwardes:

And nothing can, or shall content my Soule
Till I am eeuen'd with him, wife, for wife.
Or fayling so, yet that I put the Moore,
At least into a Ielouzie so strong
That iudgement cannot cure. Which thing to do,
If this poore Trash of Venice, whom I trace
For his quicke hunting, stand the putting on,
Ile haue our Michael Cassio on the hip,
Abuse him to the Moore, in the right garbe
(For I feare Cassio with my Night-Cape too)
Make the Moore thanke me, loue me, and reward me,
For making him egregiously an Asse,
And practising vpon his peace, and quiet,
Euen to madnesse. 'Tis heere: but yet confus'd,
Knaueries plaine face, is neuer seene, till vs'd.
Enter.

Scena Secunda.

Enter Othello's Herald with a Proclamation.

Herald. It is Othello's pleasure, our Noble and Valiant Generall. That vpon
certaine tydings now arriu'd, importing the meere perdition of the
Turkish Fleete: euery man put himselfe into Triumph. Some to daunce,
some to make Bonfires, each man, to what Sport and Reuels his addition
leads him. For besides these beneficiall Newes, it is the Celebration of his
Nuptiall. So much was his pleasure should be proclaimed. All offices are
open, & there is full libertie of Feasting from this present houre of fiue, till
the Bell haue told eleuen. Blesse the Isle of Cyprus, and our Noble
Generall Othello. Enter.

Enter Othello, Desdemona, Cassio, and Attendants.

  Othe. Good Michael, looke you to the guard to night.
Let's teach our selues that Honourable stop,
Not to out-sport discretion

  Cas. Iago, hath direction what to do.
But notwithstanding with my personall eye
Will I looke to't

Othe. Iago, is most honest:
Michael, goodnight. To morrow with your earliest,
Let me haue speech with you. Come my deere Loue,
The purchase made, the fruites are to ensue,
That profit's yet to come 'tweene me, and you.
Goodnight.
Enter.

Enter Iago.

Cas. Welcome Iago: we must to the Watch

Iago. Not this houre Lieutenant: 'tis not yet ten o'th' clocke. Our Generall cast vs thus earely for the loue of his Desdemona: Who, let vs not therefore blame; he hath not yet made wanton the night with her: and she is sport for Ioue

Cas. She's a most exquisite Lady

Iago. And Ile warrant her, full of Game

Cas. Indeed shes a most fresh and delicate creature

Iago. What an eye she ha's?
Me thinkes it sounds a parley to prouocation

Cas. An inuiting eye:
And yet me thinkes right modest

Iago. And when she speakes,
Is it not an Alarum to Loue?
Cas. She is indeed perfection

Iago. Well: happinesse to their Sheetes. Come Lieutenant, I haue a stope of Wine, and heere without are a brace of Cyprus Gallants, that would faine haue a measure to the health of blacke Othello

Cas. Not to night, good Iago, I haue very poore, and vnhappie Braines for drinking. I could well wish Curtesie would inuent some other Custome of entertainment

Iago. Oh, they are our Friends: but one Cup, Ile drinke for you

Cassio. I haue drunke but one Cup to night, and that was craftily qualified too: and behold what inouation it makes heere. I am infortunate in the infirmity, and dare not taske my weakenesse with any more

　Iago. What man? 'Tis a night of Reuels, the Gallants desire it

　Cas. Where are they?
　Iago. Heere, at the doore: I pray you call them in

　Cas. Ile do't, but it dislikes me.
Enter.

　Iago. If I can fasten but one Cup vpon him
With that which he hath drunke to night alreadie,
He'l be as full of Quarrell, and offence
As my yong Mistris dogge.
Now my sicke Foole Rodorigo,
Whom Loue hath turn'd almost the wrong side out,
To Desdemona hath to night Carrows'd.
Potations, pottle-deepe; and he's to watch.
Three else of Cyprus, Noble swelling Spirites,
(That hold their Honours in a wary distance,
The very Elements of this Warrelike Isle)
Haue I to night fluster'd with flowing Cups,
And they Watch too.
Now 'mongst this Flocke of drunkards
Am I put to our Cassio in some Action
That may offend the Isle. But here they come.
Enter Cassio, Montano, and Gentlemen.

If Consequence do but approue my dreame,
My Boate sailes freely, both with winde and Streame

Cas. 'Fore heauen, they haue giuen me a rowse already

　Mon. Good-faith a litle one: not past a pint, as I am a Souldier

　Iago. Some Wine hoa.
And let me the Cannakin clinke, clinke:
And let me the Cannakin clinke.

A Souldiers a man: Oh, mans life's but a span,
Why then let a Souldier drinke.
Some Wine Boyes

Cas. 'Fore Heauen: an excellent Song

Iago. I learn'd it in England: where indeed they are most potent in Potting.
Your Dane, your Germaine, and your swag-belly'd Hollander, (drinke hoa)
are nothing to your English

  Cassio. Is your Englishmen so exquisite in his drinking?
  Iago. Why, he drinkes you with facillitie, your Dane
dead drunke. He sweates not to ouerthrow your Almaine.
He giues your Hollander a vomit, ere the next
Pottle can be fill'd

Cas. To the health of our Generall

Mon. I am for it Lieutenant: and Ile do you Iustice

  Iago. Oh sweet England.
King Stephen was anda worthy Peere,
His Breeches cost him but a Crowne,
He held them Six pence all to deere,
With that he cal'd the Tailor Lowne:
He was a wight of high Renowne,
And thou art but of low degree:
'Tis Pride that pulls the Country downe,
And take thy awl'd Cloake about thee.
Some Wine hoa

Cassio. Why this is a more exquisite Song then the other

Iago. Will you heare't againe? Cas. No: for I hold him to be vnworthy of
his Place, that do's those things. Well: heau'ns aboue all: and there be
soules must be saued, and there be soules must not be saued

Iago. It's true, good Lieutenant

    Cas. For mine owne part, no offence to the Generall, nor any man
    of qualitie: I hope to be saued

Iago. And so do I too Lieutenant

Cassio. I: (but by your leaue) not before me. The Lieutenant is to be saued before the Ancient. Let's haue no more of this: let's to our Affaires. Forgiue vs our sinnes: Gentlemen let's looke to our businesse. Do not thinke Gentlemen, I am drunke: this is my Ancient, this is my right hand, and this is my left. I am not drunke now: I can stand well enough, and I speake well enough

Gent. Excellent well

   Cas. Why very well then: you must not thinke then,
that I am drunke.
Enter.

   Monta. To th' Platforme (Masters) come, let's set the
Watch

   Iago. You see this Fellow, that is gone before,
He's a Souldier, fit to stand by Caesar,
And giue direction. And do but see his vice,
'Tis to his vertue, a iust Equinox,
The one as long as th' other. 'Tis pittie of him:
I feare the trust Othello puts him in,
On some odde time of his infirmitie
Will shake this Island

   Mont. But is he often thus?
   Iago. 'Tis euermore his prologue to his sleepe,
He'le watch the Horologe a double Set,
If Drinke rocke not his Cradle

   Mont. It were well
The Generall were put in mind of it:
Perhaps he sees it not, or his good nature
Prizes the vertue that appeares in Cassio,
And lookes not on his euills: is not this true?
Enter Rodorigo.

   Iago. How now Rodorigo?
I pray you after the Lieutenant, go

Mon. And 'tis great pitty, that the Noble Moore
Should hazard such a Place, as his owne Second
With one of an ingraft Infirmitie,
It were an honest Action, to say so
To the Moore

Iago. Not I, for this faire Island,
I do loue Cassio well: and would do much
To cure him of this euill, But hearke, what noise?
Enter Cassio pursuing Rodorigo.

Cas. You Rogue: you Rascall

Mon. What's the matter Lieutenant?
Cas. A Knaue teach me my dutie? Ile beate the
Knaue in to a Twiggen-Bottle

Rod. Beate me?
Cas. Dost thou prate, Rogue?
Mon. Nay, good Lieutenant:
I pray you Sir, hold your hand

Cassio. Let me go (Sir)
Or Ile knocke you o're the Mazard

Mon. Come, come: you're drunke

Cassio. Drunke?
Iago. Away I say: go out and cry a Mutinie.
Nay good Lieutenant. Alas Gentlemen:
Helpe hoa. Lieutenant. Sir Montano:
Helpe Masters. Heere's a goodly Watch indeed.
Who's that which rings the Bell: Diablo, hoa:
The Towne will rise. Fie, fie Lieutenant,
You'le be asham'd for euer.
Enter Othello, and Attendants.

Othe. What is the matter heere?
Mon. I bleed still, I am hurt to th' death. He dies

Othe. Hold for your liues

Iag. Hold hoa: Lieutenant, Sir Montano, Gentlemen:
Haue you forgot all place of sense and dutie?
Hold. The Generall speakes to you: hold for shame

Oth. Why how now hoa? From whence ariseth this?
Are we turn'd Turkes? and to our selues do that
Which Heauen hath forbid the Ottamittes.
For Christian shame, put by this barbarous Brawle:
He that stirs next, to carue for his owne rage,
Holds his soule light: He dies vpon his Motion.
Silence that dreadfull Bell, it frights the Isle,
From her propriety. What is the matter, Masters?
Honest Iago, that lookes dead with greeuing,
Speake: who began this? On thy loue I charge thee?
  Iago. I do not know: Friends all, but now, euen now.
In Quarter, and in termes like Bride, and Groome
Deuesting them for Bed: and then, but now:
(As if some Planet had vnwitted men)
Swords out, and tilting one at others breastes,
In opposition bloody. I cannot speake
Any begining to this peeuish oddes.
And would, in Action glorious, I had lost
Those legges, that brought me to a part of it

Othe. How comes it (Michaell) you are thus forgot?
Cas. I pray you pardon me, I cannot speake

Othe. Worthy Montano, you were wont to be ciuill:
The grauitie, and stillnesse of your youth
The world hath noted. And your name is great
In mouthes of wisest Censure. What's the matter
That you vnlace your reputation thus,
And spend your rich opinion, for the name
Of a night-brawler? Giue me answer to it

Mon. Worthy Othello, I am hurt to danger,
Your Officer Iago, can informe you,
While I spare speech which something now offends me.
Of all that I do know, nor know I ought
By me, that's said, or done amisse this night,
Vnlesse selfe-charitie be sometimes a vice,

And to defend our selues, it be a sinne
When violence assailes vs

  Othe. Now by Heauen,
My blood begins my safer Guides to rule,
And passion (hauing my best iudgement collied)
Assaies to leade the way. If I once stir,
Or do but lift this Arme, the best of you
Shall sinke in my rebuke. Giue me to know
How this foule Rout began: Who set it on,
And he that is approu'd in this offence,
Though he had twinn'd with me, both at a birth,
Shall loose me. What in a Towne of warre,
Yet wilde, the peoples hearts brim-full of feare,
To Manage priuate, and domesticke Quarrell?
In night, and on the Court and Guard of safetie?
'Tis monstrous: Iago, who began't?
  Mon. If partially Affin'd, or league in office,
Thou dost deliuer more, or lesse then Truth,
Thou art no Souldier

  Iago. Touch me not so neere,
I had rather haue this tongue cut from my mouth,
Then it should do offence to Michaell Cassio.
Yet I perswade my selfe, to speake the truth
Shall nothing wrong him. This it is Generall:
Montano and my selfe being in speech,
There comes a Fellow, crying out for helpe,
And Cassio following him with determin'd Sword
To execute vpon him. Sir, this Gentleman,
Steppes in to Cassio, and entreats his pause:
My selfe, the crying Fellow did pursue,
Least by his clamour (as it so fell out)
The Towne might fall in fright. He, (swift of foote)
Out-ran my purpose: and I return'd then rather
For that I heard the clinke, and fall of Swords,
And Cassio high in oath: Which till to night
I nere might say before. When I came backe
(For this was briefe) I found them close together
At blow, and thrust, euen as againe they were
When you your selfe did part them.

More of this matter cannot I report,
But Men are Men: The best sometimes forget,
Though Cassio did some little wrong to him,
As men in rage strike those that wish them best,
Yet surely Cassio, I beleeue receiu'd
From him that fled, some strange Indignitie,
Which patience could not passe

  Othe. I know Iago
Thy honestie, and loue doth mince this matter,
Making it light to Cassio: Cassio, I loue thee,
But neuer more be Officer of mine.
Enter Desdemona attended.

Looke if my gentle Loue be not rais'd vp:
Ile make thee an example

  Des. What is the matter (Deere?)
  Othe. All's well, Sweeting:
Come away to bed. Sir for your hurts,
My selfe will be your Surgeon. Lead him off:
Iago, looke with care about the Towne,
And silence those whom this vil'd brawle distracted.
Come Desdemona, 'tis the Soldiers life,
To haue their Balmy slumbers wak'd with strife.
Enter.

  Iago. What are you hurt Lieutenant?
  Cas. I, past all Surgery

Iago. Marry Heauen forbid

Cas. Reputation, Reputation, Reputation: Oh I haue lost my Reputation. I
haue lost the immortall part of myselfe, and what remaines is bestiall. My
Reputation, Iago, my Reputation

Iago. As I am an honest man I had thought you had receiued some bodily
wound; there is more sence in that then in Reputation. Reputation is an
idle, and most false imposition; oft got without merit, and lost without
deseruing. You haue lost no Reputation at all, vnlesse you repute your
selfe such a looser. What man, there are more wayes to recouer the
Generall againe. You are but now cast in his moode, (a punishment more

in policie, then in malice) euen so as one would beate his offencelesse dogge, to affright an Imperious Lyon. Sue to him againe, and he's yours

Cas. I will rather sue to be despis'd, then to deceiue so good a Commander, with so slight, so drunken, and so indiscreet an Officer. Drunke? And speake Parrat? And squabble? Swagger? Sweare? And discourse Fustian with ones owne shadow? Oh thou invisible spirit of Wine, if thou hast no name to be knowne by, let vs call thee Diuell

  Iago. What was he that you follow'd with your
Sword? What had he done to you?
  Cas. I know not

Iago. Is't possible? Cas. I remember a masse of things, but nothing distinctly: a Quarrell, but nothing wherefore. Oh, that men should put an Enemie in their mouthes, to steale away their Braines? that we should with ioy, pleasance, reuell and applause, transforme our selues into Beasts

Iago. Why? But you are now well enough: how came you thus recouered? Cas. It hath pleas'd the diuell drunkennesse, to giue place to the diuell wrath, one vnperfectnesse, shewes me another to make me frankly despise my selfe

  Iago. Come, you are too seuere a Moraller. As the
Time, the Place, & the Condition of this Country stands
I could hartily wish this had not befalne: but since it is, as
it is, mend it for your owne good

Cas. I will aske him for my Place againe, he shall tell me, I am a drunkard: had I as many mouthes as Hydra, such an answer would stop them all. To be now a sensible man, by and by a Foole, and presently a Beast. Oh strange! Euery inordinate cup is vnbless'd, and the Ingredient is a diuell

  Iago. Come, come: good wine, is a good familiar
Creature, if it be well vs'd: exclaime no more against it.
And good Lieutenant, I thinke, you thinke I loue
you

Cassio. I haue well approued it, Sir. I drunke? Iago. You, or any man liuing, may be drunke at a time man. I tell you what you shall do: Our General's Wife, is now the Generall. I may say so, in this respect, for that he hath deuoted, and giuen vp himselfe to the Contemplation, marke: and deuotement of her parts and Graces. Confesse your selfe freely to her: Importune her helpe to put you in your place againe. She is of so free, so kinde, so apt, so blessed a disposition, she holds it a vice in her goodnesse, not to do more then she is requested. This broken ioynt betweene you, and her husband, entreat her to splinter. And my Fortunes against any lay worth naming, this cracke of your Loue, shall grow stronger, then it was before

Cassio. You aduise me well

   Iago. I protest in the sinceritie of Loue, and honest kindnesse

Cassio. I thinke it freely: and betimes in the morning, I will beseech the vertuous Desdemona to vndertake for me: I am desperate of my Fortunes if they check me

   Iago. You are in the right: good night Lieutenant, I must to the Watch

Cassio. Good night, honest Iago.

Exit Cassio.

  Iago. And what's he then,
That saies I play the Villaine?
When this aduise is free I giue, and honest,
Proball to thinking, and indeed the course
To win the Moore againe.
For 'tis most easie
Th' inclyning Desdemona to subdue
In any honest Suite. She's fram'd as fruitefull
As the free Elements. And then for her
To win the Moore, were to renownce his Baptisme,
All Seales, and Simbols of redeemed sin:
His Soule is so enfetter'd to her Loue,
That she may make, vnmake, do what she list,
Euen as her Appetite shall play the God,
With his weake Function. How am I then a Villaine,
To Counsell Cassio to this paralell course,
Directly to his good? Diuinitie of hell,
When diuels will the blackest sinnes put on,
They do suggest at first with heauenly shewes,

As I do now. For whiles this honest Foole
Plies Desdemona, to repaire his Fortune,
And she for him, pleades strongly to the Moore,
Ile powre this pestilence into his eare:
That she repeales him, for her bodies Lust,
And by how much she striues to do him good,
She shall vndo her Credite with the Moore.
So will I turne her vertue into pitch.
And out of her owne goodnesse make the Net,
That shall en-mash them all.
How now Rodorigo?
Enter Rodorigo.

Rodorigo. I do follow heere in the Chace, not like a Hound that hunts, but
one that filles vp the Crie. My Money is almost spent; I haue bin to night
exceedingly well Cudgell'd: And I thinke the issue will bee, I shall haue so
much experience for my paines; And so, with no money at all, and a little
more Wit, returne againe to Venice

   Iago. How poore are they that haue not Patience?
What wound did euer heale but by degrees?
Thou know'st we worke by Wit, and not by Witchcraft
And Wit depends on dilatory time:
Dos't not go well? Cassio hath beaten thee,
And thou by that small hurt hath casheer'd Cassio:
Though other things grow faire against the Sun,
Yet Fruites that blossome first, will first be ripe:
Content thy selfe, a-while. Introth 'tis Morning;
Pleasure, and Action, make the houres seeme short.
Retire thee, go where thou art Billited:
Away, I say, thou shalt know more heereafter:
Nay get thee gone.

Exit Roderigo.

Two things are to be done:
My Wife must moue for Cassio to her Mistris:
Ile set her on my selfe, a while, to draw the Moor apart,
And bring him iumpe, when he may Cassio finde
Soliciting his wife: I, that's the way:

Dull not Deuice, by coldnesse, and delay.
Enter.

Actus Tertius. Scena Prima.

Enter Cassio, Musitians, and Clowne.

  Cassio. Masters, play heere, I wil content your paines,
Something that's briefe: and bid, goodmorrow General

  Clo. Why Masters, haue your Instruments bin in Naples,
that they speake i'th' Nose thus?
  Mus. How Sir? how?
  Clo. Are these I pray you, winde Instruments?
  Mus. I marry are they sir

Clo. Oh, thereby hangs a tale

Mus. Whereby hangs a tale, sir? Clow. Marry sir, by many a winde
Instrument that I know. But Masters, heere's money for you: and the
Generall so likes your Musick, that he desires you for loues sake to make
no more noise with it

Mus. Well Sir, we will not

Clo. If you haue any Musicke that may not be heard, too't againe. But (as
they say) to heare Musicke, the Generall do's not greatly care

Mus. We haue none such, sir

  Clow. Then put vp your Pipes in your bagge, for Ile away. Go,
  vanish into ayre, away.

Exit Mu.

  Cassio. Dost thou heare me, mine honest Friend?
  Clo. No, I heare not your honest Friend:
I heare you

Cassio. Prythee keepe vp thy Quillets, ther's a poore peece of Gold for
thee: if the Gentlewoman that attends the Generall be stirring, tell her,
there's one Cassio entreats her a little fauour of Speech. Wilt thou do this?

Clo. She is stirring sir: if she will stirre hither, I shall seeme to notifie vnto her.

Exit Clo.

Enter Iago.

In happy time, Iago

  Iago. You haue not bin a-bed then?
  Cassio. Why no: the day had broke before we parted.
I haue made bold (Iago) to send in to your wife:
My suite to her is, that she will to vertuous Desdemona
Procure me some accesse

  Iago. Ile send her to you presently:
And Ile deuise a meane to draw the Moore
Out of the way, that your conuerse and businesse
May be more free.

Exit

  Cassio. I humbly thanke you for't. I neuer knew
A Florentine more kinde, and honest.
Enter aemilia.

Aemil. Goodmorrow (good Lieutenant) I am sorrie
For your displeasure: but all will sure be well.
The Generall and his wife are talking of it,
And she speakes for you stoutly. The Moore replies,
That he you hurt is of great Fame in Cyprus,
And great Affinitie: and that in wholsome Wisedome
He might not but refuse you. But he protests he loues you
And needs no other Suitor, but his likings
To bring you in againe

  Cassio. Yet I beseech you,
If you thinke fit, or that it may be done,
Giue me aduantage of some breefe Discourse
With Desdemon alone.
Aemil. Pray you come in:

I will bestow you where you shall haue time
To speake your bosome freely

Cassio. I am much bound to you.

Scoena Secunda.

Enter Othello, Iago, and Gentlemen.

  Othe. These Letters giue (Iago) to the Pylot,
And by him do my duties to the Senate:
That done, I will be walking on the Workes,
Repaire there to mee

Iago. Well, my good Lord, Ile doo't

  Oth. This Fortification (Gentlemen) shall we see't?
  Gent. Well waite vpon your Lordship.

Exeunt.

Scoena Tertia.

Enter Desdemona, Cassio, and aemilia.

  Des. Be thou assur'd (good Cassio) I will do
All my abilities in thy behalfe.
Aemil. Good Madam do:
I warrant it greeues my Husband,
As if the cause were his

  Des. Oh that's an honest Fellow, Do not doubt Cassio
But I will haue my Lord, and you againe
As friendly as you were

  Cassio. Bounteous Madam,
What euer shall become of Michael Cassio,
He's neuer any thing but your true Seruant

  Des. I know't: I thanke you: you do loue my Lord:
You haue knowne him long, and be you well assur'd
He shall in strangenesse stand no farther off,
Then in a politique distance

Cassio. I, but Lady,
That policie may either last so long,
Or feede vpon such nice and waterish diet,
Or breede it selfe so out of Circumstances,
That I being absent, and my place supply'd,
My Generall will forget my Loue, and Seruice

Des. Do not doubt that: before aemilia here,
I giue thee warrant of thy place. Assure thee,
If I do vow a friendship, Ile performe it
To the last Article. My Lord shall neuer rest,
Ile watch him tame, and talke him out of patience;
His Bed shall seeme a Schoole, his Boord a Shrift,
Ile intermingle euery thing he do's
With Cassio's suite: Therefore be merry Cassio,
For thy Solicitor shall rather dye,
Then giue thy cause away.
Enter Othello, and Iago.

Aemil. Madam, heere comes my Lord

Cassio. Madam, Ile take my leaue

Des. Why stay, and heare me speake

Cassio. Madam, not now: I am very ill at ease,
Vnfit for mine owne purposes

Des. Well, do your discretion.

Exit Cassio.

Iago. Hah? I like not that

Othel. What dost thou say?
Iago. Nothing my Lord; or if- I know not what

Othel. Was not that Cassio parted from my wife?
Iago. Cassio my Lord? No sure, I cannot thinke it
That he would steale away so guilty-like,
Seeing your comming

Oth. I do beleeue 'twas he

  Des. How now my Lord?
I haue bin talking with a Suitor heere,
A man that languishes in your displeasure

  Oth. Who is't you meane?
  Des. Why your Lieutenant Cassio: Good my Lord,
If I haue any grace, or power to moue you,
His present reconciliation take.
For if he be not one, that truly loues you,
That erres in Ignorance, and not in Cunning,
I haue no iudgement in an honest face.
I prythee call him backe

  Oth. Went he hence now?
  Des. I sooth; so humbled,
That he hath left part of his greefe with mee
To suffer with him. Good Loue, call him backe

Othel. Not now (sweet Desdemon) some other time

  Des. But shall't be shortly?
  Oth. The sooner (Sweet) for you

  Des. Shall't be to night, at Supper?
  Oth. No, not to night

  Des. To morrow Dinner then?
  Oth. I shall not dine at home:
I meete the Captaines at the Cittadell

  Des. Why then to morrow night, on Tuesday morne,
On Tuesday noone, or night; on Wensday Morne.
I prythee name the time, but let it not
Exceed three dayes. Infaith hee's penitent:
And yet his Trespasse, in our common reason
(Saue that they say the warres must make example)
Out of her best, is not almost a fault
T' encurre a priuate checke. When shall he come?
Tell me Othello. I wonder in my Soule
What you would aske me, that I should deny,

Or stand so mam'ring on? What? Michael Cassio,
That came a woing with you? and so many a time
(When I haue spoke of you dispraisingly)
Hath tane your part, to haue so much to do
To bring him in? Trust me, I could do much

   Oth. Prythee no more: Let him come when he will:
I will deny thee nothing

   Des. Why, this is not a Boone:
'Tis as I should entreate you weare your Gloues,
Or feede on nourishing dishes, or keepe you warme,
Or sue to you, to do a peculiar profit
To your owne person. Nay, when I haue a suite
Wherein I meane to touch your Loue indeed,
It shall be full of poize, and difficult waight,
And fearefull to be granted

   Oth. I will deny thee nothing.
Whereon, I do beseech thee, grant me this,
To leaue me but a little to my selfe

Des. Shall I deny you? No: farewell my Lord

Oth. Farewell my Desdemona, Ile come to thee strait

   Des. aemilia come; be as your Fancies teach you:
What ere you be, I am obedient.
Enter.

   Oth. Excellent wretch: Perdition catch my Soule
But I do loue thee: and when I loue thee not,
Chaos is come againe

Iago. My Noble Lord

   Oth. What dost thou say, Iago?
   Iago. Did Michael Cassio
When he woo'd my Lady, know of your loue?
   Oth. He did, from first to last:
Why dost thou aske?

Iago. But for a satisfaction of my Thought,
No further harme

Oth. Why of thy thought, Iago?
Iago. I did not thinke he had bin acquainted with hir

Oth. O yes, and went betweene vs very oft

Iago. Indeed?
Oth. Indeed? I indeed. Discern'st thou ought in that?
Is he not honest?
Iago. Honest, my Lord?
Oth. Honest? I, Honest

Iago. My Lord, for ought I know

Oth. What do'st thou thinke?
Iago. Thinke, my Lord?
Oth. Thinke, my Lord? Alas, thou ecchos't me;
As if there were some Monster in thy thought
Too hideous to be shewne. Thou dost mean somthing:
I heard thee say euen now, thou lik'st not that,
When Cassio left my wife. What didd'st not like?
And when I told thee, he was of my Counsaile,
Of my whole course of wooing; thou cried'st, Indeede?
And didd'st contract, and purse thy brow together,
As if thou then hadd'st shut vp in thy Braine
Some horrible Conceite. If thou do'st loue me,
Shew me thy thought

Iago. My Lord, you know I loue you

Oth. I thinke thou do'st:
And for I know thou'rt full of Loue, and Honestie,
And weigh'st thy words before thou giu'st them breath,
Therefore these stops of thine, fright me the more:
For such things in a false disloyall Knaue
Are trickes of Custome: but in a man that's iust,
They're close dilations, working from the heart,
That Passion cannot rule

Iago. For Michael Cassio,
I dare be sworne, I thinke that he is honest

Oth. I thinke so too

Iago. Men should be what they seeme,
Or those that be not, would they might seeme none

Oth. Certaine, men should be what they seeme

Iago. Why then I thinke Cassio's an honest man

Oth. Nay, yet there's more in this?
I prythee speake to me, as to thy thinkings,
As thou dost ruminate, and giue thy worst of thoughts
The worst of words

Iago. Good my Lord pardon me,
Though I am bound to euery Acte of dutie,
I am not bound to that: All Slaues are free:
Vtter my Thoughts? Why say, they are vild, and falce?
As where's that Palace, whereinto foule things
Sometimes intrude not? Who ha's that breast so pure,
Wherein vncleanly Apprehensions
Keepe Leetes, and Law-dayes, and in Sessions sit
With meditations lawfull?
Oth. Thou do'st conspire against thy Friend (Iago)
If thou but think'st him wrong'd, and mak'st his eare
A stranger to thy Thoughts

Iago. I do beseech you,
Though I perchance am vicious in my guesse
(As I confesse it is my Natures plague
To spy into Abuses, and of my iealousie
Shapes faults that are not) that your wisedome
From one, that so imperfectly conceits,
Would take no notice, nor build your selfe a trouble
Out of his scattering, and vnsure obseruance:
It were not for your quiet, nor your good,
Nor for my Manhood, Honesty, and Wisedome,
To let you know my thoughts

Oth. What dost thou meane?

Iago. Good name in Man, & woman (deere my Lord)
Is the immediate Iewell of their Soules;
Who steales my purse, steales trash:
'Tis something, nothing;
'Twas mine, 'tis his, and has bin slaue to thousands:
But he that filches from me my good Name,
Robs me of that, which not enriches him,
And makes me poore indeed

Oth. Ile know thy Thoughts

Iago. You cannot, if my heart were in your hand,
Nor shall not, whil'st 'tis in my custodie

Oth. Ha?

Iago. Oh, beware my Lord, of iealousie,
It is the greene-ey'd Monster, which doth mocke
The meate it feeds on. That Cuckold liues in blisse,
Who certaine of his Fate, loues not his wronger:
But oh, what damned minutes tels he ore,
Who dotes, yet doubts: Suspects, yet soundly loues?

Oth. O miserie

Iago. Poore, and Content, is rich, and rich enough,
But Riches finelesse, is as poore as Winter,
To him that euer feares he shall be poore:
Good Heauen, the Soules of all my Tribe defend
From Iealousie

Oth. Why? why is this?
Think'st thou, I'ld make a Life of Iealousie;
To follow still the changes of the Moone
With fresh suspitions? No: to be once in doubt,
Is to be resolu'd: Exchange me for a Goat,
When I shall turne the businesse of my Soule
To such exufflicate, and blow'd Surmises,
Matching thy inference. 'Tis not to make me Iealious,
To say my wife is faire, feeds well, loues company,
Is free of Speech, Sings, Playes, and Dances:
Where Vertue is, these are more vertuous.

Nor from mine owne weake merites, will I draw
The smallest feare, or doubt of her reuolt,
For she had eyes, and chose me. No Iago,
Ile see before I doubt; when I doubt, proue;
And on the proofe, there is no more but this,
Away at once with Loue, or Iealousie

  Ia. I am glad of this: For now I shall haue reason
To shew the Loue and Duty that I beare you
With franker spirit. Therefore (as I am bound)
Receiue it from me. I speake not yet of proofe:
Looke to your wife, obserue her well with Cassio,
Weare your eyes, thus: not Iealious, nor Secure:
I would not haue your free, and Noble Nature,
Out of selfe-Bounty, be abus'd: Looke too't:
I know our Country disposition well:
In Venice, they do let Heauen see the prankes
They dare not shew their Husbands.
Their best Conscience,
Is not to leaue't vndone, but kept vnknowne

  Oth. Dost thou say so?
  Iago. She did deceiue her Father, marrying you,
And when she seem'd to shake, and feare your lookes,
She lou'd them most

Oth. And so she did

  Iago. Why go too then:
Shee that so young could giue out such a Seeming
To seele her Fathers eyes vp, close as Oake,
He thought 'twas Witchcraft.
But I am much too blame:
I humbly do beseech you of your pardon
For too much louing you

Oth. I am bound to thee for euer

  Iago. I see this hath a little dash'd your Spirits:
  Oth. Not a iot, not a iot

Iago. Trust me, I feare it has:
I hope you will consider what is spoke
Comes from your Loue.
But I do see y'are moou'd:
I am to pray you, not to straine my speech
To grosser issues, nor to larger reach,
Then to Suspition

Oth. I will not

Iago. Should you do so (my Lord)
My speech should fall into such vilde successe,
Which my Thoughts aym'd not.
Cassio's my worthy Friend:
My Lord, I see y'are mou'd

Oth. No, not much mou'd:
I do not thinke but Desdemona's honest

Iago. Long liue she so;
And long liue you to thinke so

Oth. And yet how Nature erring from it selfe

Iago. I, there's the point:
As (to be bold with you)
Not to affect many proposed Matches
Of her owne Clime, Complexion, and Degree,
Whereto we see in all things, Nature tends:
Foh, one may smel in such, a will most ranke,
Foule disproportions, Thoughts vnnaturall.
But (pardon me) I do not in position
Distinctly speake of her, though I may feare
Her will, recoyling to her better iudgement,
May fal to match you with her Country formes,
And happily repent

Oth. Farewell, farewell:
If more thou dost perceiue, let me know more:
Set on thy wife to obserue.
Leaue me Iago

Iago. My Lord, I take my leaue

   Othel. Why did I marry?
This honest Creature (doubtlesse)
Sees, and knowes more, much more then he vnfolds

   Iago. My Lord, I would I might intreat your Honor
To scan this thing no farther: Leaue it to time,
Although 'tis fit that Cassio haue his Place;
For sure he filles it vp with great Ability;
Yet if you please, to him off a-while:
You shall by that perceiue him, and his meanes:
Note if your Lady straine his Entertainment
With any strong, or vehement importunitie,
Much will be seene in that: In the meane time,
Let me be thought too busie in my feares,
(As worthy cause I haue to feare I am)
And hold her free, I do beseech your Honor

Oth. Feare not my gouernment

   Iago. I once more take my leaue.
Enter.

   Oth. This Fellow's of exceeding honesty,
And knowes all Quantities with a learn'd Spirit
Of humane dealings. If I do proue her Haggard,
Though that her Iesses were my deere heart-strings,
I'ld whistle her off, and let her downe the winde
To prey at Fortune. Haply, for I am blacke,
And haue not those soft parts of Conuersation
That Chamberers haue: Or for I am declin'd
Into the vale of yeares (yet that's not much)
Shee's gone. I am abus'd, and my releefe
Must be to loath her. Oh Curse of Marriage!
That we can call these delicate Creatures ours,
And not their Appetites? I had rather be a Toad,
And liue vpon the vapour of a Dungeon,
Then keepe a corner in the thing I loue
For others vses. Yet 'tis the plague to Great-ones,
Prerogatiu'd are they lesse then the Base,

'Tis destiny vnshunnable, like death:
Euen then, this forked plague is Fated to vs,
When we do quicken. Looke where she comes:
Enter Desdemona and aemilia.

If she be false, Heauen mock'd it selfe:
Ile not beleeue't

  Des. How now, my deere Othello?
Your dinner, and the generous Islanders
By you inuited, do attend your presence

Oth. I am too blame

  Des. Why do you speake so faintly?
Are you not well?
  Oth. I haue a paine vpon my Forehead, heere

  Des. Why that's with watching, 'twill away againe.
Let me but binde it hard, within this houre
It will be well

  Oth. Your Napkin is too little:
Let it alone: Come, Ile go in with you.
Enter.

  Des. I am very sorry that you are not well.
Aemil. I am glad I haue found this Napkin:
This was her first remembrance from the Moore,
My wayward Husband hath a hundred times
Woo'd me to steale it. But she so loues the Token,
(For he coniur'd her, she should euer keepe it)
That she reserues it euermore about her,
To kisse, and talke too. Ile haue the worke tane out,
And giu't Iago: what he will do with it
Heauen knowes, not I:
I nothing, but to please his Fantasie.
Enter Iago.

  Iago. How now? What do you heere alone?
Aemil. Do not you chide: I haue a thing for you

Iago. You haue a thing for me?
It is a common thing-
Aemil. Hah?
  Iago. To haue a foolish wife.
Aemil. Oh, is that all? What will you giue me now
For that same Handkerchiefe

  Iago. What Handkerchiefe?
Aemil. What Handkerchiefe?
Why that the Moore first gaue to Desdemona,
That which so often you did bid me steale

  Iago. Hast stolne it from her?
Aemil. No: but she let it drop by negligence,
And to th' aduantage, I being heere, took't vp:
Looke, heere 'tis

  Iago. A good wench, giue it me.
Aemil. What will you do with't, that you haue bene
so earnest to haue me filch it?
  Iago. Why, what is that to you?
Aemil. If it be not for some purpose of import,
Giu't me againe. Poore Lady, shee'l run mad
When she shall lacke it

  Iago. Be not acknowne on't:
I haue vse for it. Go, leaue me.

Exit aemil.

I will in Cassio's Lodging loose this Napkin,
And let him finde it. Trifles light as ayre,
Are to the iealious, confirmations strong,
As proofes of holy Writ. This may do something.
The Moore already changes with my poyson:
Dangerous conceites, are in their Natures poysons,
Which at the first are scarse found to distaste:
But with a little acte vpon the blood,
Burne like the Mines of Sulphure. I did say so.
Enter Othello.

Looke where he comes: Not Poppy, nor Mandragora,
Nor all the drowsie Syrrups of the world
Shall euer medicine thee to that sweete sleepe
Which thou owd'st yesterday

  Oth. Ha, ha, false to mee?
  Iago. Why how now Generall? No more of that

  Oth. Auant, be gone: Thou hast set me on the Racke:
I sweare 'tis better to be much abus'd,
Then but to know't a little

  Iago. How now, my Lord?
  Oth. What sense had I, in her stolne houres of Lust?
I saw't not, thought it not: it harm'd not me:
I slept the next night well, fed well, was free, and merrie.
I found not Cassio's kisses on her Lippes:
He that is robb'd, not wanting what is stolne,
Let him not know't, and he's not robb'd at all

  Iago. I am sorry to heare this?
  Oth. I had beene happy, if the generall Campe,
Pyoners and all, had tasted her sweet Body,
So I had nothing knowne. Oh now, for euer
Farewell the Tranquill minde; farewell Content;
Farewell the plumed Troopes, and the bigge Warres,
That makes Ambition, Vertue! Oh farewell,
Farewell the neighing Steed, and the shrill Trumpe,
The Spirit-stirring Drum, th' Eare-piercing Fife,
The Royall Banner, and all Qualitie,
Pride, Pompe, and Circumstance of glorious Warre:
And O you mortall Engines, whose rude throates
Th' immortall Ioues dread Clamours, counterfet,
Farewell: Othello's Occupation's gone

  Iago. Is't possible my Lord?
  Oth. Villaine, be sure thou proue my Loue a Whore;
Be sure of it: Giue me the Occular proofe,
Or by the worth of mine eternall Soule,
Thou had'st bin better haue bin borne a Dog
Then answer my wak'd wrath

Iago. Is't come to this?

Oth. Make me to see't: or (at the least) so proue it,
That the probation beare no Hindge, nor Loope,
To hang a doubt on: Or woe vpon thy life

Iago. My Noble Lord

Oth. If thou dost slander her, and torture me,
Neuer pray more: Abandon all remorse
On Horrors head, Horrors accumulate:
Do deeds to make Heauen weepe, all Earth amaz'd;
For nothing canst thou to damnation adde,
Greater then that

Iago. O Grace! O Heauen forgiue me!
Are you a Man? Haue you a Soule? or Sense?
God buy you: take mine Office. Oh wretched Foole,
That lou'st to make thine Honesty, a Vice!
Oh monstrous world! Take note, take note (O World)
To be direct and honest, is not safe.
I thanke you for this profit, and from hence
Ile loue no Friend, sith Loue breeds such offence

Oth. Nay stay: thou should'st be honest

Iago. I should be wise; for Honestie's a Foole,
And looses that it workes for

Oth. By the World,
I thinke my Wife be honest, and thinke she is not:
I thinke that thou art iust, and thinke thou art not:
Ile haue some proofe. My name that was as fresh
As Dians Visage, is now begrim'd and blacke
As mine owne face. If there be Cords, or Kniues,
Poyson, or Fire, or suffocating streames,
Ile not indure it. Would I were satisfied

Iago. I see you are eaten vp with Passion:
I do repent me, that I put it to you.
You would be satisfied?

Oth. Would? Nay, and I will

Iago. And may: but how? How satisfied, my Lord?
Would you the super-vision grossely gape on?
Behold her top'd?
  Oth. Death, and damnation. Oh!
  Iago. It were a tedious difficulty, I thinke,
To bring them to that Prospect: Damne them then,
If euer mortall eyes do see them boulster
More then their owne. What then? How then?
What shall I say? Where's Satisfaction?
It is impossible you should see this,
Were they as prime as Goates, as hot as Monkeyes,
As salt as Woules in pride, and Fooles as grosse
As Ignorance, made drunke. But yet, I say,
If imputation, and strong circumstances,
Which leade directly to the doore of Truth,
Will giue you satisfaction, you might haue't

Oth. Giue me a liuing reason she's disloyall

  Iago. I do not like the Office.
But sith I am entred in this cause so farre
(Prick'd too't by foolish Honesty, and Loue)
I will go on. I lay with Cassio lately,
And being troubled with a raging tooth,
I could not sleepe. There are a kinde of men,
So loose of Soule, that in their sleepes will mutter
Their Affayres: one of this kinde is Cassio:
In sleepe I heard him say, sweet Desdemona,
Let vs be wary, let vs hide our Loues,
And then (Sir) would he gripe, and wring my hand:
Cry, oh sweet Creature: then kisse me hard,
As if he pluckt vp kisses by the rootes,
That grew vpon my lippes, laid his Leg ore my Thigh,
And sigh, and kisse, and then cry cursed Fate,
That gaue thee to the Moore

  Oth. O monstrous! monstrous!
  Iago. Nay, this was but his Dreame

  Oth. But this denoted a fore-gone conclusion,
'Tis a shrew'd doubt, though it be but a Dreame

Iago. And this may helpe to thicken other proofes,
That do demonstrate thinly

Oth. Ile teare her all to peeces

Iago. Nay yet be wise; yet we see nothing done,
She may be honest yet: Tell me but this,
Haue you not sometimes seene a Handkerchiefe
Spotted with Strawberries, in your wiues hand?
  Oth. I gaue her such a one: 'twas my first gift

Iago. I know not that: but such a Handkerchiefe
(I am sure it was your wiues) did I to day
See Cassio wipe his Beard with

Oth. If it be that

Iago. If it be that, or any, it was here.
It speakes against her with the other proofes

Othel. O that the Slaue had forty thousand liues:
One is too poore, too weake for my reuenge.
Now do I see 'tis true. Looke heere Iago,
All my fond loue thus do I blow to Heauen. 'Tis gone.
Arise blacke vengeance, from the hollow hell,
Yeeld vp (O Loue) thy Crowne, and hearted Throne
To tyrannous Hate. Swell bosome with thy fraught,
For 'tis of Aspickes tongues

Iago. Yet be content

Oth. Oh blood, blood, blood

Iago. Patience I say: your minde may change

Oth. Neuer Iago. Like to the Ponticke Sea,
Whose Icie Current, and compulsiue course,
Neu'r keepes retyring ebbe, but keepes due on
To the Proponticke, and the Hellespont:
Euen so my bloody thoughts, with violent pace
Shall neu'r looke backe, neu'r ebbe to humble Loue,
Till that a capeable, and wide Reuenge

Swallow them vp. Now by yond Marble Heauen,
In the due reuerence of a Sacred vow,
I heere engage my words

  Iago. Do not rise yet:
Witnesse you euer-burning Lights aboue,
You Elements, that clip vs round about,
Witnesse that heere Iago doth giue vp
The execution of his wit, hands, heart,
To wrong'd Othello's Seruice. Let him command,
And to obey shall be in me remorse,
What bloody businesse euer

  Oth. I greet thy loue,
Not with vaine thanks, but with acceptance bounteous,
And will vpon the instant put thee too't.
Within these three dayes let me heare thee say,
That Cassio's not aliue

  Iago. My Friend is dead:
'Tis done at your Request.
But let her liue

  Oth. Damne her lewde Minx:
O damne her, damne her.
Come go with me a-part, I will withdraw
To furnish me with some swift meanes of death
For the faire Diuell.
Now art thou my Lieutenant

Iago. I am your owne for euer.

Exeunt.

Scaena Quarta.

Enter Desdemona, aemilia, and Clown.

  Des. Do you know Sirrah, where Lieutenant Cassio
lyes?
  Clow. I dare not say he lies any where

Des. Why man?
Clo. He's a Soldier, and for me to say a Souldier lyes,
'tis stabbing

Des. Go too: where lodges he?
Clo. To tell you where he lodges, is to tel you where
I lye

Des. Can any thing be made of this?
Clo. I know not where he lodges, and for mee to deuise
a lodging, and say he lies heere, or he lies there, were
to lye in mine owne throat

Des. Can you enquire him out? and be edified by report?
Clo. I will Catechize the world for him, that is, make
Questions, and by them answer

Des. Seeke him, bidde him come hither: tell him, I haue moou'd my Lord
on his behalfe, and hope all will be well

Clo. To do this, is within the compasse of mans Wit,
and therefore I will attempt the doing it.

Exit Clo.

Des. Where should I loose the Handkerchiefe, aemilia?
Aemil. I know not Madam

Des. Beleeue me, I had rather haue lost my purse
Full of Cruzadoes. And but my Noble Moore
Is true of minde, and made of no such basenesse,
As iealious Creatures are, it were enough
To put him to ill-thinking.
Aemil. Is he not iealious?
Des. Who, he? I thinke the Sun where he was borne,
Drew all such humors from him.
Aemil. Looke where he comes.
Enter Othello.

Des. I will not leaue him now, till Cassio be
Call'd to him. How is't with you, my Lord?
Oth. Well my good Lady. Oh hardnes to dissemble!

How do you, Desdemona?
  Des. Well, my good Lord

  Oth. Giue me your hand.
This hand is moist, my Lady

Des. It hath felt no age, nor knowne no sorrow

  Oth. This argues fruitfulnesse, and liberall heart:
Hot, hot, and moyst. This hand of yours requires
A sequester from Liberty: Fasting, and Prayer,
Much Castigation, Exercise deuout,
For heere's a yong, and sweating Diuell heere
That commonly rebels: 'Tis a good hand,
A franke one

  Des. You may (indeed) say so:
For 'twas that hand that gaue away my heart

  Oth. A liberall hand. The hearts of old, gaue hands:
But our new Heraldry is hands, not hearts

  Des. I cannot speake of this:
Come, now your promise

  Oth. What promise, Chucke?
  Des. I haue sent to bid Cassio come speake with you

  Oth. I haue a salt and sorry Rhewme offends me:
Lend me thy Handkerchiefe

Des. Heere my Lord

Oth. That which I gaue you

Des. I haue it not about me

  Oth. Not?
  Des. No indeed, my Lord

  Oth. That's a fault: That Handkerchiefe
Did an aegyptian to my Mother giue:
She was a Charmer, and could almost read

The thoughts of people. She told her, while she kept it,
'T would make her Amiable, and subdue my Father
Intirely to her loue: But if she lost it,
Or made a Guift of it, my Fathers eye
Should hold her loathed, and his Spirits should hunt
After new Fancies. She dying, gaue it me,
And bid me (when my Fate would haue me Wiu'd)
To giue it her. I did so; and take heede on't,
Make it a Darling, like your precious eye:
To loose't, or giue't away, were such perdition,
As nothing else could match

  Des. Is't possible?
  Oth. 'Tis true: There's Magicke in the web of it:
A Sybill that had numbred in the world
The Sun to course, two hundred compasses,
In her Prophetticke furie sow'd the Worke:
The Wormes were hallowed, that did breede the Silke,
And it was dyde in Mummey, which the Skilfull
Conseru'd of Maidens hearts

  Des. Indeed? Is't true?
  Oth. Most veritable, therefore looke too't well

  Des. Then would to Heauen, that I had neuer seene't?
  Oth. Ha? wherefore?
  Des. Why do you speake so startingly, and rash?
  Oth. Is't lost? Is't gon? Speak, is't out o'th' way?
  Des. Blesse vs

  Oth. Say you?
  Des. It is not lost: but what and if it were?
  Oth. How?
  Des. I say it is not lost

Oth. Fetcht, let me see't

  Des. Why so I can: but I will not now:
This is a tricke to put me from my suite,
Pray you let Cassio be receiu'd againe

Oth. Fetch me the Handkerchiefe,
My minde mis-giues

Des. Come, come: you'l neuer meete a more sufficient
man

Oth. The Handkerchiefe

Des. A man that all his time
Hath founded his good Fortunes on your loue;
Shar'd dangers with you

Oth. The Handkerchiefe

Des. Insooth, you are too blame

Oth. Away.

Exit Othello.

Aemil. Is not this man iealious?
  Des. I neu'r saw this before.
Sure, there's some wonder in this Handkerchiefe,
I am most vnhappy in the losse of it.
Aemil. 'Tis not a yeare or two shewes vs a man:
They are all but Stomackes, and we all but Food,
They eate vs hungerly, and when they are full
They belch vs.
Enter Iago, and Cassio.

Looke you, Cassio and my Husband

  Iago. There is no other way: 'tis she must doo't:
And loe the happinesse: go, and importune her

  Des. How now (good Cassio) what's the newes with
you?
  Cassio. Madam, my former suite. I do beseech you,
That by your vertuous meanes, I may againe
Exist, and be a member of his loue,
Whom I, with all the Office of my heart
Intirely honour, I would not be delayd.

If my offence, be of such mortall kinde,
That nor my Seruice past, nor present Sorrowes,
Nor purpos'd merit in futurity,
Can ransome me into his loue againe,
But to know so, must be my benefit:
So shall I cloath me in a forc'd content,
And shut my selfe vp in some other course
To Fortunes Almes

  Des. Alas (thrice-gentle Cassio)
My Aduocation is not now in Tune;
My Lord, is not my Lord; nor should I know him,
Were he in Fauour, as in Humour alter'd.
So helpe me euery spirit sanctified,
As I haue spoken for you all my best,
And stood within the blanke of his displeasure
For my free speech. You must awhile be patient:
What I can do, I will: and more I will
Then for my selfe, I dare. Let that suffice you

  Iago. Is my Lord angry?
Aemil. He went hence but now:
And certainly in strange vnquietnesse

  Iago. Can he be angry? I haue seen the Cannon
When it hath blowne his Rankes into the Ayre,
And like the Diuell from his very Arme
Puff't his owne Brother: And is he angry?
Something of moment then: I will go meet him,
There's matter in't indeed, if he be angry.

Exit

  Des. I prythee do so. Something sure of State,
Either from Venice, or some vnhatch'd practise
Made demonstrable heere in Cyprus, to him,
Hath pudled his cleare Spirit: and in such cases,
Mens Natures wrangle with inferiour things,
Though great ones are their obiect. 'Tis euen so.
For let our finger ake, and it endues
Our other healthfull members, euen to a sense

Of paine. Nay, we must thinke men are not Gods,
Nor of them looke for such obseruancie
As fits the Bridall. Beshrew me much, aemilia,
I was (vnhandsome Warrior, as I am)
Arraigning his vnkindnesse with my soule:
But now I finde, I had suborn'd the Witnesse,
And he's Indited falsely.
Aemil. Pray heauen it bee
State matters, as you thinke, and no Conception,
Nor no Iealious Toy, concerning you

  Des. Alas the day, I neuer gaue him cause.
Aemil. But Iealious soules will not be answer'd so;
They are not euer iealious for the cause,
But iealious, for they're iealious. It is a Monster
Begot vpon it selfe, borne on it selfe

  Des. Heauen keepe the Monster from Othello's mind.
Aemil. Lady, Amen

  Des. I will go seeke him. Cassio, walke heere about:
If I doe finde him fit, Ile moue your suite,
And seeke to effect it to my vttermost.

Exit

  Cas. I humbly thanke your Ladyship.
Enter Bianca.

  Bian. 'Saue you (Friend Cassio.)
  Cassio. What make you from home?
How is't with you, my most faire Bianca?
Indeed (sweet Loue) I was comming to your house

  Bian. And I was going to your Lodging, Cassio.
What? keepe a weeke away? Seuen dayes, and Nights?
Eight score eight houres? And Louers absent howres
More tedious then the Diall, eight score times?
Oh weary reck'ning

  Cassio. Pardon me, Bianca:
I haue this while with leaden thoughts beene prest,

But I shall in a more continuate time
Strike off this score of absence. Sweet Bianca
Take me this worke out

   Bianca. Oh Cassio, whence came this?
This is some Token from a newer Friend,
To the felt-Absence: now I feele a Cause:
Is't come to this? Well, well

   Cassio. Go too, woman:
Throw your vilde gesses in the Diuels teeth,
From whence you haue them. You are iealious now,
That this is from some Mistris, some remembrance;
No, in good troth Bianca

   Bian. Why, who's is it?
   Cassio. I know not neither:
I found it in my Chamber,
I like the worke well; Ere it be demanded
(As like enough it will) I would haue it coppied:
Take it, and doo't, and leaue me for this time

   Bian. Leaue you? Wherefore?
   Cassio. I do attend heere on the Generall,
And thinke it no addition, nor my wish
To haue him see me woman'd

   Bian. Why, I pray you?
   Cassio. Not that I loue you not

   Bian. But that you do not loue me.
I pray you bring me on the way a little,
And say, if I shall see you soone at night?
   Cassio. 'Tis but a little way that I can bring you,
For I attend heere: But Ile see you soone

Bian. 'Tis very good: I must be circumstanc'd.

Exeunt. omnes.

Actus Quartus. Scena Prima.

Enter Othello, and Iago.

Iago. Will you thinke so?
Oth. Thinke so, Iago?
Iago. What, to kisse in priuate?
Oth. An vnauthoriz'd kisse?
Iago. Or to be naked with her Friend in bed,
An houre, or more, not meaning any harme?
Oth. Naked in bed (Iago) and not meane harme?
It is hypocrisie against the Diuell:
They that meane vertuously, and yet do so,
The Diuell their vertue tempts, and they tempt Heauen

Iago. If they do nothing, 'tis a Veniall slip:
But if I giue my wife a Handkerchiefe

Oth. What then?
Iago. Why then 'tis hers (my Lord) and being hers,
She may (I thinke) bestow't on any man

Oth. She is Protectresse of her honor too:
May she giue that?
Iago. Her honor is an Essence that's not seene,
They haue it very oft, that haue it not.
But for the Handkerchiefe

Othe. By heauen, I would most gladly haue forgot it:
Thou saidst (oh, it comes ore my memorie,
As doth the Rauen o're the infectious house:
Boading to all) he had my Handkerchiefe

Iago . I: what of that?
Othe. That's not so good now

Iag. What if I had said, I had seene him do you wrong?
Or heard him say (as Knaues be such abroad,
Who hauing by their owne importunate suit,
Or voluntary dotage of some Mistris,
Conuinced or supply'd them, cannot chuse
But they must blab.)
Oth. Hath he said any thing?

Iago. He hath (my Lord) but be you well assur'd,
No more then he'le vn-sweare

Oth. What hath he said?
Iago. Why, that he did: I know not what he did

Othe. What? What?
Iago. Lye

Oth. With her?
Iago. With her? On her: what you will

Othe. Lye with her? lye on her? We say lye on her, when they be-lye-her.
Lye with her: that's fullsome: Handkerchiefe: Confessions: Handkerchiefe.
To confesse, and be hang'd for his labour. First, to be hang'd, and then to
confesse: I tremble at it. Nature would not inuest her selfe in such
shadowing passion, without some Instruction. It is not words that shakes
me thus, (pish) Noses, Eares, and Lippes: is't possible. Confesse?
Handkerchiefe? O diuell.

Falls in a Traunce.

Iago. Worke on,
My Medicine workes. Thus credulous Fooles are caught,
And many worthy, and chast Dames euen thus,
(All guiltlesse) meete reproach: what hoa? My Lord?
My Lord, I say: Othello.
Enter Cassio.

How now Cassio?
Cas. What's the matter?
Iago. My Lord is falne into an Epilepsie,
This is his second Fit: he had one yesterday

Cas. Rub him about the Temples

Iago. The Lethargie must haue his quyet course:
If not, he foames at mouth: and by and by
Breakes out to sauage madnesse. Looke, he stirres:
Do you withdraw your selfe a little while,
He will recouer straight: when he is gone,
I would on great occasion, speake with you.

How is it Generall? Haue you not hurt your head?

Othe. Dost thou mocke me?

Iago. I mocke you not, by Heauen:
Would you would beare your Fortune like a Man

Othe. A Horned man's a Monster, and a Beast

Iago. Ther's many a Beast then in a populous Citty,
And many a ciuill Monster

Othe. Did he confesse it?

Iago. Good Sir, be a man:
Thinke euery bearded fellow that's but yoak'd
May draw with you. There's Millions now aliue,
That nightly lye in those vnproper beds,
Which they dare sweare peculiar. Your case is better.
Oh, 'tis the spight of hell, the Fiends Arch-mock,
To lip a wanton in a secure Cowch;
And to suppose her chast. No, let me know,
And knowing what I am, I know what she shallbe

Oth. Oh, thou art wise: 'tis certaine

Iago. Stand you a while apart,
Confine your selfe but in a patient List,
Whil'st you were heere, o're-whelmed with your griefe
(A passion most resulting such a man)
Cassio came hither: I shifted him away,
And layd good scuses vpon your Extasie,
Bad him anon returne: and heere speake with me,
The which he promis'd. Do but encaue your selfe,
And marke the Fleeres, the Gybes, and notable Scornes
That dwell in euery Region of his face.
For I will make him tell the Tale anew;
Where, how, how oft, how long ago, and when
He hath, and is againe to cope your wife.
I say, but marke his gesture: marry Patience,
Or I shall say y'are all in all in Spleene,
And nothing of a man

Othe. Do'st thou heare, Iago,
I will be found most cunning in my Patience:
But (do'st thou heare) most bloody

Iago. That's not amisse,
But yet keepe time in all: will you withdraw?
Now will I question Cassio of Bianca,
A Huswife that by selling her desires
Buyes her selfe Bread, and Cloath. It is a Creature
That dotes on Cassio, (as 'tis the Strumpets plague
To be-guile many, and be be-guil'd by one)
He, when he heares of her, cannot restraine
From the excesse of Laughter. Heere he comes.
Enter Cassio.

As he shall smile, Othello shall go mad:
And his vnbookish Ielousie must conserue
Poore Cassio's smiles, gestures, and light behauiours
Quite in the wrong. How do you Lieutenant?
  Cas. The worser, that you giue me the addition,
Whose want euen killes me

Iago. Ply Desdemona well, and you are sure on't:
Now, if this Suit lay in Bianca's dowre,
How quickely should you speed?
  Cas. Alas poore Caitiffe

Oth. Looke how he laughes already

Iago. I neuer knew woman loue man so

Cas. Alas poore Rogue, I thinke indeed she loues me

Oth. Now he denies it faintly: and laughes it out

Iago. Do you heare Cassio?
  Oth. Now he importunes him
To tell it o're: go too, well said, well said

Iago. She giues it out, that you shall marry her.
Do you intend it?
  Cas. Ha, ha, ha

Oth. Do ye triumph, Romaine? do you triumph?

Cas. I marry. What? A customer; prythee beare
Some Charitie to my wit, do not thinke it
So vnwholesome. Ha, ha, ha

Oth. So, so, so, so: they laugh, that winnes

Iago. Why the cry goes, that you marry her

Cas. Prythee say true

Iago. I am a very Villaine else

Oth. Haue you scoar'd me? Well

Cas. This is the Monkeys owne giuing out:
She is perswaded I will marry her
Out of her owne loue & flattery, not out of my promise

Oth. Iago becomes me: now he begins the story

Cassio. She was heere euen now: she haunts me in euery place. I was the
other day talking on the Seabanke with certaine Venetians, and thither
comes the Bauble, and falls me thus about my neck

Oth. Crying oh deere Cassio, as it were: his iesture imports
it

Cassio. So hangs, and lolls, and weepes vpon me:
So shakes, and pulls me. Ha, ha, ha

Oth. Now he tells how she pluckt him to my Chamber: oh, I see that nose
of yours, but not that dogge, I shall throw it to

Cassio. Well, I must leaue her companie

Iago. Before me: looke where she comes.
Enter Bianca.

Cas. 'Tis such another Fitchew: marry a perfum'd one? What do you
meane by this haunting of me? Bian. Let the diuell, and his dam haunt
you: what did you meane by that same Handkerchiefe, you gaue me euen
now? I was a fine Foole to take it: I must take out the worke? A likely

piece of worke, that you should finde it in your Chamber, and know not who left it there. This is some Minxes token, & I must take out the worke? There, giue it your Hobbey-horse, wheresoeuer you had it, Ile take out no worke on't

  Cassio. How now, my sweete Bianca?
How now? How now?
  Othe. By Heauen, that should be my Handkerchiefe

  Bian. If you'le come to supper to night you may, if you will not come when you are next prepar'd for.

Exit

Iago. After her: after her

Cas. I must, shee'l rayle in the streets else

  Iago. Will you sup there?
  Cassio. Yes, I intend so

  Iago. Well, I may chance to see you: for I would very faine speake with you

  Cas. Prythee come: will you?
  Iago. Go too; say no more

Oth. How shall I murther him, Iago

  Iago. Did you perceiue how he laugh'd at his vice?
  Oth. Oh, Iago

  Iago. And did you see the Handkerchiefe?
  Oth. Was that mine?
  Iago. Yours by this hand: and to see how he prizes the foolish woman your wife: she gaue it him and, he hath giu'n it his whore

  Oth. I would haue him nine yeeres a killing:
A fine woman, a faire woman, a sweete woman?
  Iago. Nay, you must forget that

Othello. I, let her rot and perish, and be damn'd to night, for she shall not liue. No, my heart is turn'd to stone: I strike it, and it hurts my hand. Oh, the world hath not a sweeter Creature: she might lye by an Emperours side, and command him Taskes

Iago. Nay, that's not your way

Othe. Hang her, I do but say what she is: so delicate with her Needle: an admirable Musitian. Oh she will sing the Sauagenesse out of a Beare: of so high and plenteous wit, and inuention? Iago. She's the worse for all this

Othe. Oh, a thousand, a thousand times:
And then of so gentle a condition?
Iago. I too gentle

Othe. Nay that's certaine:
But yet the pitty of it, Iago: oh Iago, the pitty of it
Iago

Iago. If you are so fond ouer her iniquitie: giue her pattent to offend, for if it touch not you, it comes neere no body

Oth. I will chop her into Messes: Cuckold me?
Iago. Oh, 'tis foule in her

Oth. With mine Officer?
Iago. That's fouler

Othe. Get me some poyson, Iago, this night. Ile not expostulate with her: least her body and beautie vnprouide my mind againe: this night Iago

Iago. Do it not with poyson, strangle her in her bed,
Euen the bed she hath contaminated

Oth. Good, good:
The Iustice of it pleases: very good

Iago. And for Cassio, let me be his vndertaker:
You shall heare more by midnight.
Enter Lodouico, Desdemona, and Attendants.

Othe. Excellent good: What Trumpet is that same?
Iago. I warrant something from Venice,

'Tis Lodouico, this, comes from the Duke.
See, your wife's with him

Lodo. Saue you worthy Generall

Othe. With all my heart Sir

Lod. The Duke, and the Senators of Venice greet you

Othe. I kisse the Instrument of their pleasures

  Des. And what's the newes, good cozen Lodouico
  Iago. I am very glad to see you Signior:
Welcome to Cyprus

  Lod. I thanke you: how do's Lieutenant Cassio?
  Iago. Liues Sir,
  Des. Cozen, there's falne betweene him, & my Lord,
An vnkind breach: but you shall make all well

  Othe. Are you sure of that?
  Des. My Lord?
  Othe. This faile you not to do, as you will-
  Lod. He did not call: he's busie in the paper,
Is there deuision 'twixt my Lord, and Cassio?
  Des. A most vnhappy one: I would do much
T' attone, them, for the loue I beare to Cassio

Oth. Fire, and brimestone

Des. My Lord

  Oth. Are you wise?
  Des. What is he angrie?
  Lod. May be the Letter mou'd him.
For as I thinke, they do command him home,
Deputing Cassio in his Gouernment

Des. Trust me, I am glad on't

  Othe. Indeed?
  Des. My Lord?
  Othe. I am glad to see you mad

Des. Why, sweete Othello?
Othe. Diuell

Des. I haue not deseru'd this

Lod. My Lord, this would not be beleeu'd in Venice,
Though I should sweare I saw't. 'Tis very much,
Make her amends: she weepes

Othe. Oh diuell, diuell:
If that the Earth could teeme with womans teares,
Each drop she falls, would proue a Crocodile:
Out of my sight

Des. I will not stay to offend you

Lod. Truely obedient Lady:
I do beseech your Lordship call her backe

Othe. Mistris

Des. My Lord

Othe. What would you with her, Sir?
Lod. Who I, my Lord?
Othe. I, you did wish, that I would make her turne:
Sir, she can turne, and turne: and yet go on
And turne againe. And she can weepe, Sir, weepe.
And she's obedient: as you say obedient.
Very obedient: proceed you in your teares.
Concerning this Sir, (oh well-painted passion)
I am commanded home: get you away:
Ile send for you anon. Sir I obey the Mandate,
And will returne to Venice. Hence, auaunt:
Cassio shall haue my Place. And Sir, to night
I do entreat, that we may sup together.
You are welcome Sir to Cyprus.
Goates, and Monkeys.
Enter.

Lod. Is this the Noble Moore, whom our full Senate
Call all in all sufficient? Is this the Nature

Whom Passion could not shake? Whose solid vertue
The shot of Accident, nor dart of Chance
Could neither graze, nor pierce?
  Iago. He is much chang'd

  Lod. Are his wits safe? Is he not light of Braine?
  Iago. He's that he is: I may not breath my censure.
What he might be: if what he might, he is not,
I would to heauen he were

  Lod. What? Strike his wife?
  Iago. 'Faith that was not so well: yet would I knew
That stroke would proue the worst

  Lod. Is it his vse?
Or did the Letters, worke vpon his blood,
And new create his fault?
  Iago. Alas, alas:
It is not honestie in me to speake
What I haue seene, and knowne. You shall obserue him,
And his owne courses will denote him so,
That I may saue my speech: do but go after
And marke how he continues

Lod. I am sorry that I am deceiu'd in him.

Exeunt.

Scena Secunda.

Enter Othello and aemilia.

  Othe. You haue seene nothing then?
Aemil. Nor euer heard: nor euer did suspect

Othe. Yes, you haue seene Cassio, and she together

  Aemi. But then I saw no harme: and then I heard,
Each syllable that breath made vp betweene them

  Othe. What? Did they neuer whisper?
Aemil. Neuer my Lord

Othe. Nor send you out o'th' way?
Aemil. Neuer

Othe. To fetch her Fan, her Gloues, her Mask, nor nothing?
Aemil. Neuer my Lord

Othe. That's strange.
Aemil. I durst (my Lord) to wager, she is honest:
Lay downe my Soule at stake: If you thinke other,
Remoue your thought. It doth abuse your bosome:
If any wretch haue put this in your head,
Let Heauen requit it with the Serpents curse,
For if she be not honest, chaste, and true,
There's no man happy. The purest of their Wiues
Is foule as Slander

Othe. Bid her come hither: go.

Exit aemilia.

She saies enough: yet she's a simple Baud
That cannot say as much. This is a subtile Whore:
A Closset Locke and Key of Villanous Secrets,
And yet she'le kneele, and pray: I haue seene her do't.
Enter Desdemona, and aemilia.

  Des. My Lord, what is your will?
  Othe. Pray you Chucke come hither

  Des. What is your pleasure?
  Oth. Let me see your eyes: looke in my face

  Des. What horrible Fancie's this?
  Othe. Some of your Function Mistris:
Leaue Procreants alone, and shut the doore:
Cough, or cry hem; if any body come:
Your Mystery, your Mystery: May dispatch.

Exit aemi.

  Des. Vpon my knee, what doth your speech import?
I vnderstand a Fury in your words

Othe. Why? What art thou?
Des. Your wife my Lord: your true and loyall wife

Othello. Come sweare it: damne thy selfe, least being like one of Heauen,
the diuells themselues should feare to ceaze thee. Therefore be double
damn'd: sweare thou art honest

Des. Heauen doth truely know it

Othe. Heauen truely knowes, that thou art false as hell

  Des. To whom my Lord?
With whom? How am I false?
  Othe. Ah Desdemon, away, away, away

  Des. Alas the heauy day: why do you weepe?
Am I the motiue of these teares my Lord?
If happely you my Father do suspect,
An Instrument of this your calling backe,
Lay not your blame on me: if you haue lost him,
I haue lost him too

  Othe. Had it pleas'd Heauen,
To try me with Affliction, had they rain'd
All kind of Sores, and Shames on my bare-head:
Steep'd me in pouertie to the very lippes.
Giuen to Captiuitie, me, and my vtmost hopes,
I should haue found in some place of my Soule
A drop of patience. But alas, to make me
The fixed Figure for the time of Scorne,
To point his slow, and mouing finger at.
Yet could I beare that too, well, very well:
But there where I haue garnerd vp my heart,
Where either I must liue, or beare no life,
The Fountaine from the which my currant runnes,
Or else dries vp: to be discarded thence,
Or keepe it as a Cesterne, for foule Toades
To knot and gender in. Turne thy complexion there:
Patience, thou young and Rose-lip'd Cherubin,
I heere looke grim as hell

Des. I hope my Noble Lord esteemes me honest

Othe. Oh I, as Sommer Flyes are in the Shambles,
That quicken euen with blowing. Oh thou weed:
Who art so louely faire, and smell'st so sweete,
That the Sense akes at thee,
Would thou had'st neuer bin borne

Des. Alas, what ignorant sin haue I committed?
Othe. Was this faire Paper? This most goodly Booke
Made to write Whore vpon? What commited,
Committed? Oh, thou publicke Commoner,
I should make very Forges of my cheekes,
That would to Cynders burne vp Modestie,
Did I but speake thy deedes. What commited?
Heauen stoppes the Nose at it, and the Moone winks:
The baudy winde that kisses all it meetes,
Is hush'd within the hollow Myne of Earth
And will not hear't. What commited?
Des. By Heauen you do me wrong

Othe. Are not you a Strumpet?
Des. No, as I am a Christian.
If to preserue this vessell for my Lord,
From any other foule vnlawfull touch
Be not to be a Strumpet, I am none

Othe. What, not a Whore?
Des. No, as I shall be sau'd

Othe. Is't possible?
Des. Oh Heauen forgiue vs

Othe. I cry you mercy then.
I tooke you for that cunning Whore of Venice,
That married with Othello. You Mistris,
Enter aemilia.

That haue the office opposite to Saint Peter,
And keepes the gate of hell. You, you: I you.
We haue done our course: there's money for your paines:
I pray you turne the key, and keepe our counsaile.
Enter.

Aemil. Alas, what do's this Gentleman conceiue?
How do you Madam? how do you my good Lady?
  Des. Faith, halfe a sleepe

  Aemi. Good Madam,
What's the matter with my Lord?
  Des. With who?
Aemil. Why, with my Lord, Madam?
  Des. Who is thy Lord?
Aemil. He that is yours, sweet Lady

  Des. I haue none: do not talke to me, aemilia,
I cannot weepe: nor answeres haue I none,
But what should go by water. Prythee to night,
Lay on my bed my wedding sheetes, remember,
And call thy husband hither.
Aemil. Heere's a change indeed.
Enter.

  Des. 'Tis meete I should be vs'd so: very meete.
How haue I bin behau'd, that he might sticke
The small'st opinion on my least misvse?
Enter Iago, and aemilia.

  Iago. What is your pleasure Madam?
How is't with you?
  Des. I cannot tell: those that do teach yong Babes
Do it with gentle meanes, and easie taskes.
He might haue chid me so; for in good faith
I am a Child to chiding

  Iago. What is the matter Lady?
Aemil. Alas (Iago) my Lord hath so bewhor'd her,
Throwne such dispight, and heauy termes vpon her
That true hearts cannot beare it

  Des. Am I that name, Iago?
  Iago. What name, (faire Lady?)
  Des. Such as she said my Lord did say I was.
Aemil. He call'd her whore: a Begger in his drinke:
Could not haue laid such termes vpon his Callet

Iago. Why did he so?
Des. I do not know: I am sure I am none such

Iago. Do not weepe, do not weepe: alas the day.
Aemil. Hath she forsooke so many Noble Matches?
Her Father? And her Country? And her Friends?
To be call'd Whore? Would it not make one weepe?
Des. It is my wretched Fortune

Iago. Beshrew him for't:
How comes this Tricke vpon him?
Des. Nay, Heauen doth know

Aemi. I will be hang'd, if some eternall Villaine,
Some busie and insinuating Rogue,
Some cogging, cozening Slaue, to get some Office,
Haue not deuis'd this Slander: I will be hang'd else

Iago. Fie, there is no such man: it is impossible

Des. If any such there be, Heauen pardon him.
Aemil. A halter pardon him:
And hell gnaw his bones.
Why should he call her Whore?
Who keepes her companie?
What Place? What Time?
What Forme? What liklyhood?
The Moore's abus'd by some most villanous Knaue,
Some base notorious Knaue, some scuruy Fellow.
Oh Heauens, that such companions thou'd'st vnfold,
And put in euery honest hand a whip
To lash the Rascalls naked through the world,
Euen from the East to th' West

Iago. Speake within doore.
Aemil. Oh fie vpon them: some such Squire he was
That turn'd your wit, the seamy-side without,
And made you to suspect me with the Moore

Iago. You are a Foole: go too

Des. Alas Iago,
What shall I do to win my Lord againe?
Good Friend, go to him: for by this light of Heauen,
I know not how I lost him. Heere I kneele:
If ere my will did trespasse 'gainst his Loue,
Either in discourse of thought, or actuall deed,
Or that mine Eyes, mine Eares, or any Sence
Delighted them: or any other Forme.
Or that I do not yet, and euer did,
And euer will, (though he do shake me off
To beggerly diuorcement) Loue him deerely,
Comfort forsweare me. Vnkindnesse may do much,
And his vnkindnesse may defeat my life,
But neuer taynt my Loue. I cannot say Whore,
It do's abhorre me now I speake the word,
To do the Act, that might the addition earne,
Not the worlds Masse of vanitie could make me

   Iago. I pray you be content: 'tis but his humour:
The businesse of the State do's him offence

Des. If 'twere no other

   Iago. It is but so, I warrant,
Hearke how these Instruments summon to supper:
The Messengers of Venice staies the meate,
Go in, and weepe not: all things shall be well.

Exeunt. Desdemona and aemilia.

Enter Rodorigo.

How now Rodorigo?
   Rod. I do not finde
That thou deal'st iustly with me

Iago. What in the contrarie? Rodori. Euery day thou dafts me with some
deuise Iago, and rather, as it seemes to me now, keep'st from me all
conueniencie, then suppliest me with the least aduantage of hope: I will
indeed no longer endure it. Nor am I yet perswaded to put vp in peace,
what already I haue foolishly suffred

Iago. Will you heare me Rodorigo?

Rodori. I haue heard too much: and your words and
Performances are no kin together

Iago. You charge me most vniustly

Rodo. With naught but truth: I haue wasted my selfe out of my meanes.
The Iewels you haue had from me to deliuer Desdemona, would halfe
haue corrupted a Votarist. You haue told me she hath receiu'd them, and
return'd me expectations and comforts of sodaine respect, and
acquaintance, but I finde none

Iago. Well, go too: very well

Rod. Very well, go too: I cannot go too, (man) nor 'tis not very well. Nay I
think it is scuruy: and begin to finde my selfe fopt in it

Iago. Very well

Rodor. I tell you, 'tis not very well: I will make my selfe knowne to
Desdemona. If she will returne me my Iewels, I will giue ouer my Suit, and
repent my vnlawfull solicitation. If not, assure your selfe, I will seeke
satisfaction of you

Iago. You haue said now

Rodo. I: and said nothing but what I protest intendment of doing

Iago. Why, now I see there's mettle in thee: and euen from this instant do
build on thee a better opinion then euer before: giue me thy hand
Rodorigo. Thou hast taken against me a most iust exception: but yet I
protest I haue dealt most directly in thy Affaire

Rod. It hath not appeer'd

Iago. I grant indeed it hath not appeer'd: and your suspition is not without
wit and iudgement. But Rodorigo, if thou hast that in thee indeed, which I
haue greater reason to beleeue now then euer (I meane purpose, Courage,
and Valour) this night shew it. If thou the next night following enioy not
Desdemona, take me from this world with Treacherie, and deuise Engines
for my life

Rod. Well: what is it? Is it within, reason and compasse?

Iago. Sir, there is especiall Commission come from
Venice to depute Cassio in Othello's place

Rod. Is that true? Why then Othello and Desdemona
returne againe to Venice

Iago. Oh no: he goes into Mauritania and taketh away with him the faire
Desdemona, vnlesse his abode be lingred heere by some accident.
Wherein none can be so determinate, as the remouing of Cassio

Rod. How do you meane remouing him?

Iago. Why, by making him vncapable of Othello's
place: knocking out his braines

Rod. And that you would haue me to do

Iago. I: if you dare do your selfe a profit, and a right. He sups to night with
a Harlotry: and thither will I go to him. He knowes not yet of his
Honourable Fortune, if you will watch his going thence (which I will
fashion to fall out betweene twelue and one) you may take him at your
pleasure. I will be neere to second your Attempt, and he shall fall
betweene vs. Come, stand not amaz'd at it, but go along with me: I will
shew you such a necessitie in his death, that you shall thinke your selfe
bound to put it on him. It is now high supper time: and the night growes
to wast. About it

Rod. I will heare further reason for this

Iago. And you shalbe satisfi'd.

Exeunt.

Scena Tertia.

Enter Othello, Lodouico, Desdemona, aemilia, and Atendants.

Lod. I do beseech you Sir, trouble your selfe no further

Oth. Oh pardon me: 'twill do me good to walke

Lodoui. Madam, good night: I humbly thanke your
Ladyship

Des. Your Honour is most welcome

Oth. Will you walke Sir? Oh Desdemona

Des. My Lord

   Othello. Get you to bed on th' instant, I will be return'd
forthwith: dismisse your Attendant there: look't
be done.
Enter.

Des. I will my Lord

Aem. How goes it now? He lookes gentler then he did

   Des. He saies he will returne incontinent,
And hath commanded me to go to bed,
And bid me to dismisse you

   Aemi. Dismisse me?
  Des. It was his bidding: therefore good aemilia,
Giue me my nightly wearing, and adieu.
We must not now displease him.
Aemil. I, would you had neuer seene him

   Des. So would not I: my loue doth so approue him,
That euen his stubbornesse, his checks, his frownes,
(Prythee vn-pin me) haue grace and fauour

Aemi. I haue laid those Sheetes you bad me on the bed

   Des. All's one: good Father, how foolish are our minds?
If I do die before, prythee shrow'd me
In one of these same Sheetes.
Aemil. Come, come: you talke

   Des. My Mother had a Maid call'd Barbarie,
She was in loue: and he she lou'd prou'd mad,
And did forsake her. She had a Song of Willough,
An old thing 'twas: but it express'd her Fortune,

And she dy'd singing it. That Song to night,
Will not go from my mind: I haue much to do,
But to go hang my head all at one side
And sing it like poore Barbarie: prythee dispatch

  Aemi. Shall I go fetch your Night-gowne?
  Des. No, vn-pin me here,
This Lodouico is a proper man.
Aemil. A very handsome man

Des. He speakes well. Aemil. I know a Lady in Venice would haue walk'd
barefoot to Palestine for a touch of his nether lip

  Des. The poore Soule sat singing, by a Sicamour tree.
Sing all a greene Willough:
Her hand on her bosome her head on her knee,
Sing Willough, Willough, Willough.
The fresh Streames ran by her, and murmur'd her moanes
Sing Willough, &c.
Her salt teares fell from her, and softned the stones,
Sing Willough, &c. (Lay by these)
Willough, Willough. (Prythee high thee: he'le come anon)
Sing all a greene Willough must be my Garland.
Let no body blame him, his scorne I approue.
(Nay that's not next. Harke, who is't that knocks?
Aemil. It's the wind

  Des. I call'd my Loue false Loue: but what said he then?
Sing Willough, &c.
If I court mo women, you'le couch with mo men.
So get thee gone, good night: mine eyes do itch:
Doth that boade weeping?
Aemil. 'Tis neyther heere, nor there

  Des. I haue heard it said so. O these Men, these men!
Do'st thou in conscience thinke (tell me aemilia)
That there be women do abuse their husbands
In such grosse kinde?
Aemil. There be some such, no question

Des. Would'st thou do such a deed for all the world?

Aemil. Why, would not you?

Des. No, by this Heauenly light.

Aemil. Nor I neither, by this Heauenly light:
I might doo't as well i'th' darke

Des. Would'st thou do such a deed for al the world?

Aemil. The world's a huge thing:
It is a great price, for a small vice

Des. Introth, I thinke thou would'st not. Aemil. Introth I thinke I should, and vndoo't when I had done. Marry, I would not doe such a thing for a ioynt Ring, nor for measures of Lawne, nor for Gownes, Petticoats, nor Caps, nor any petty exhibition. But for all the whole world: why, who would not make her husband a Cuckold, to make him a Monarch? I should venture Purgatory for't

Des. Beshrew me, if I would do such a wrong For the whole world. Aemil. Why, the wrong is but a wrong i'th' world; and hauing the world for your labour, 'tis a wrong in your owne world, and you might quickly make it right

Des. I do not thinke there is any such woman.

Aemil. Yes, a dozen: and as many to'th' vantage, as
would store the world they plaid for.
But I do thinke it is their Husbands faults
If Wiues do fall: (Say, that they slacke their duties,
And powre our Treasures into forraigne laps;
Or else breake out in peeuish Iealousies,
Throwing restraint vpon vs: Or say they strike vs,
Or scant our former hauing in despight)
Why we haue galles: and though we haue some Grace,
Yet haue we some Reuenge. Let Husbands know,
Their wiues haue sense like them: They see, and smell,
And haue their Palats both for sweet, and sowre,
As Husbands haue. What is it that they do,
When they change vs for others? Is it Sport?
I thinke it is: and doth Affection breed it?
I thinke it doth. Is't Frailty that thus erres?
It is so too. And haue not we Affections?
Desires for Sport? and Frailty, as men haue?

Then let them vse vs well: else let them know,
The illes we do, their illes instruct vs so

  Des. Good night, good night:
Heauen me such vses send,
Not to picke bad, from bad; but by bad, mend.

Exeunt.

Actus Quintus. Scena Prima.

Enter Iago, and Rodorigo.

  Iago. Heere, stand behinde this Barke,
Straight will he come:
Weare thy good Rapier bare, and put it home:
Quicke, quicke, feare nothing; Ile be at thy Elbow,
It makes vs, or it marres vs, thinke on that,
And fixe most firme thy Resolution

Rod. Be neere at hand, I may miscarry in't

Iago. Heere, at thy hand: Be bold, & take thy stand

  Rod. I haue no great deuotion to the deed,
And yet he hath giuen me satisfying Reasons:
'Tis but a man gone. Forth my Sword: he dies

  Iago. I haue rub'd this yong Quat almost to the sense,
And he growes angry. Now, whether he kill Cassio,
Or Cassio him, or each do kill the other,
Euery way makes my gaine. Liue Rodorigo,
He calles me to a restitution large
Of Gold, and Iewels, that I bob'd from him,
As Guifts to Desdemona.
It must not be: If Cassio do remaine,
He hath a dayly beauty in his life,
That makes me vgly: and besides, the Moore
May vnfold me to him: there stand I in much perill:
No, he must dye. But so, I heard him comming.
Enter Cassio.

Rod. I know his gate, 'tis he: Villaine thou dyest

  Cas. That thrust had beene mine enemy indeed,
But that my Coate is better then thou know'st:
I will make proofe of thine

Rod. Oh, I am slaine

  Cassio. I am maym'd for euer:
Helpe hoa: Murther, murther.
Enter Othello.

Oth. The voyce of Cassio. Iago keepes his word

Rod. O Villaine that I am

Oth. It is euen so

Cas. Oh helpe hoa: Light, a Surgeon

  Oth. 'Tis he: O braue Iago, honest, and iust,
That hast such Noble sense of thy Friends wrong,
Thou teachest me. Minion, your deere lyes dead,
And your vnblest Fate highes: Strumpet I come:
For of my heart, those Charmes thine Eyes, are blotted.
Thy Bed lust-stain'd, shall with Lusts blood bee spotted.

Exit Othello.

Enter Lodouico and Gratiano.

  Cas. What hoa? no Watch? No passage?
Murther, Murther

Gra. 'Tis some mischance, the voyce is very direfull

Cas. Oh helpe

Lodo. Hearke

Rod. Oh wretched Villaine

Lod. Two or three groane. 'Tis heauy night;
These may be counterfeits: Let's think't vnsafe
To come into the cry, without more helpe

Rod. Nobody come: then shall I bleed to death.
Enter Iago.

Lod. Hearke

Gra. Here's one comes in his shirt, with Light, and
Weapons

Iago. Who's there?
Who's noyse is this that cries on murther?
Lodo. We do not know

Iago. Do not you heare a cry?
Cas. Heere, heere: for heauen sake helpe me

Iago. What's the matter?
Gra. This is Othello's Ancient, as I take it

Lodo. The same indeede, a very valiant Fellow

Iago. What are you heere, that cry so greeuously?
Cas. Iago? Oh I am spoyl'd, vndone by Villaines:
Giue me some helpe

Iago. O mee, Lieutenant!
What Villaines haue done this?
Cas. I thinke that one of them is heereabout.
And cannot make away

Iago. Oh treacherous Villaines:
What are you there? Come in, and giue some helpe

Rod. O helpe me there

Cassio. That's one of them

Iago. Oh murd'rous Slaue! O Villaine!
Rod. O damn'd Iago! O inhumane Dogge!
Iago. Kill men i'th' darke?

Where be these bloody Theeues?
How silent is this Towne? Hoa, murther, murther.
What may you be? Are you of good, or euill?
  Lod. As you shall proue vs, praise vs

  Iago. Signior Lodouico?
Lod. He Sir

Iago. I cry you mercy: here's Cassio hurt by Villaines

  Gra. Cassio?
  Iago. How is't Brother?
  Cas. My Legge is cut in two

  Iago. Marry heauen forbid:
Light Gentlemen, Ile binde it with my shirt.
Enter Bianca.

  Bian. What is the matter hoa? Who is't that cry'd?
  Iago. Who is't that cry'd?
  Bian. Oh my deere Cassio,
My sweet Cassio: Oh Cassio, Cassio, Cassio

  Iago. O notable Strumpet. Cassio, may you suspect
Who they should be, that haue thus mangled you?
  Cas. No

  Gra. I am sorry to finde you thus;
I haue beene to seeke you

  Iago. Lend me a Garter. So: - Oh for a Chaire
To beare him easily hence

Bian. Alas he faints. Oh Cassio, Cassio, Cassio

  Iago. Gentlemen all, I do suspect this Trash
To be a party in this Iniurie.
Patience awhile, good Cassio. Come, come;
Lend me a Light: know we this face, or no?
Alas my Friend, and my deere Countryman
Rodorigo? No: Yes sure: Yes, 'tis Rodorigo

Gra. What, of Venice?

Iago. Euen he Sir: Did you know him?

Gra. Know him? I

Iago. Signior Gratiano? I cry your gentle pardon:
These bloody accidents must excuse my Manners,
That so neglected you

Gra. I am glad to see you

Iago. How do you Cassio? Oh, a Chaire, a Chaire

Gra. Rodorigo?

Iago. He, he, 'tis he:
Oh that's well said, the Chaire.
Some good man beare him carefully from hence,
Ile fetch the Generall's Surgeon. For you Mistris,
Saue you your labour. He that lies slaine heere (Cassio)
Was my deere friend. What malice was between you

Cas. None in the world: nor do I know the man?

Iago. What? looke you pale? Oh beare him o'th' Ayre.
Stay you good Gentlemen. Looke you pale, Mistris?
Do you perceiue the gastnesse of her eye?
Nay, if you stare, we shall heare more anon.
Behold her well: I pray you looke vpon her:
Do you see Gentlemen? Nay, guiltinesse will speake
Though tongues were out of vse.

Aemil. Alas, what is the matter?
What is the matter, Husband?

Iago. Cassio hath heere bin set on in the darke
By Rodorigo, and Fellowes that are scap'd:
He's almost slaine, and Rodorigo quite dead.

Aemil. Alas good Gentleman: alas good Cassio

Iago. This is the fruits of whoring. Prythe aemilia,
Go know of Cassio where he supt to night.
What, do you shake at that?

Bian. He supt at my house, but I therefore shake not

Iago. O did he so? I charge you go with me.

Aemil. Oh fie vpon thee Strumpet

Bian. I am no Strumpet, but of life as honest,
As you that thus abuse me.
Aemil. As I? Fie vpon thee

Iago. Kinde Gentlemen:
Let's go see poore Cassio drest.
Come Mistris, you must tel's another Tale.
aemilia, run you to the Cittadell,
And tell my Lord and Lady, what hath happ'd:
Will you go on afore? This is the night
That either makes me, or foredoes me quight.

Exeunt.

Scoena Secunda.

Enter Othello, and Desdemona in her bed.

Oth. It is the Cause, it is the Cause (my Soule)
Let me not name it to you, you chaste Starres,
It is the Cause. Yet Ile not shed her blood,
Nor scarre that whiter skin of hers, then Snow,
And smooth as Monumentall Alablaster:
Yet she must dye, else shee'l betray more men:
Put out the Light, and then put out the Light:
If I quench thee, thou flaming Minister,
I can againe thy former light restore,
Should I repent me. But once put out thy Light,
Thou cunning'st Patterne of excelling Nature,
I know not where is that Promethaean heate
That can thy Light re-Lume.
When I haue pluck'd thy Rose,
I cannot giue it vitall growth againe,
It needs must wither. Ile smell thee on the Tree.
Oh Balmy breath, that dost almost perswade
Iustice to breake her Sword. One more, one more:
Be thus when thou art dead, and I will kill thee,
And loue thee after. One more, and that's the last.
So sweet, was ne're so fatall. I must weepe,
But they are cruell Teares: This sorrow's heauenly,
It strikes, where it doth loue. She wakes

Des. Who's there? Othello?
Othel. I Desdemona

Des. Will you come to bed, my Lord?
Oth. Haue you pray'd to night, Desdemon?
Des. I my Lord

Oth. If you bethinke your selfe of any Crime
Vnreconcil'd as yet to Heauen, and Grace,
Solicite for it straight

Des. Alacke, my Lord,
What may you meane by that?
Oth. Well, do it, and be breefe, I will walke by:
I would not kill thy vnprepared Spirit,
No, Heauens fore-fend) I would not kill thy Soule

Des. Talke you of killing?
Oth. I, I do

Des. Then Heauen haue mercy on mee

Oth. Amen, with all my heart

Des. If you say, I hope you will not kill me

Oth. Humh

Des. And yet I feare you: for you're fatall then
When your eyes rowle so.
Why I should feare, I know not,
Since guiltinesse I know not: But yet I feele I feare

Oth. Thinke on thy sinnes

Des. They are Loues I beare to you

Oth. I, and for that thou dy'st

Des. That death's vnnaturall, that kils for louing.
Alas, why gnaw you so your nether-lip?
Some bloody passion shakes your very Frame:

These are portents: but yet I hope, I hope,
They do not point on me

Oth. Peace, and be still

  Des. I will so: What's the matter?
  Oth. That Handkerchiefe
Which I so lou'd, and gaue thee, thou gau'st to Cassio

  Des. No by my Life, and Soule: send for the man,
And aske him

  Oth. Sweet Soule, take heed, take heed of Periury,
Thou art on thy death-bed

Des. I, but not yet to dye

  Oth. Presently.
Therefore confesse thee freely of thy sinne:
For to deny each Article with Oath,
Cannot remoue, nor choake the strong Conception
That I do grone withall. Thou art to dye

Des. O Heauen haue mercy on me

Oth. I say, Amen

  Des. And haue you mercy too. I neuer did
Offend you in my life: neuer lou'd Cassio,
But with such generall warrantie of Heauen,
As I might loue. I neuer gaue him Token

  Oth. By Heauen I saw my Handkerchiefe in's hand.
O periur'd woman, thou do'st stone my heart,
And makes me call, what I intend to do,
A Murther, which I thought a Sacrifice.
I saw the Handkerchiefe

  Des. He found it then:
I neuer gaue it him: Send, for him hither:
Let him confesse a truth

Oth. He hath confest

Des. What, my Lord?
Oth. That he hath vs'd thee

Des. How? vnlawfully?
Oth. I

Des. He will not say so

Oth. No: his mouth is stopp'd:
Honest Iago hath 'tane order for't

Des. Oh, my feare interprets. What is he dead?
Oth. Had all his haires bin liues, my great Reuenge
Had stomacke for them all

Des. Alas, he is betray'd, and I vndone

Oth. Out Strumpet: weep'st thou for him to my face?
Des. O banish me, my Lord, but kill me not

Oth. Downe Strumpet

Des. Kill me to morrow, let me liue to night

Oth. Nay, if you striue

Des. But halfe an houre

Oth. Being done, there is no pawse

Des. But while I say one prayer

Oth. It is too late.

Smothers her.

aemilia at the doore.

Aemil. My Lord, my Lord? What hoa?
My Lord, my Lord

Oth. What noise is this? Not dead? not yet quite dead?
I that am cruell, am yet mercifull,

I would not haue thee linger in thy paine?
So, so.
Aemil. within. What hoa? my Lord, my Lord?
 Oth. Who's there?
Aemil. Oh good my Lord, I would speake a word
with you

   Oth. Yes: 'Tis aemilia: by and by. Shee's dead.
'Tis like she comes to speake of Cassio's death:
The noise was high. Hah, no more moouing?
Still as the Graue. Shall she come in? Wer't good?
I thinke she stirres againe. No, what's best to do?
If she come in, shee'l sure speake to my wife:
My wife, my wife: what wife? I haue no wife.
Oh insupportable! Oh heauy houre!
Me thinkes, it should be now a huge Eclipse
Of Sunne, and Moone; and that th' affrighted Globe
Did yawne at Alteration.
Aemil. I do beseech you
That I may speake with you. Oh good my Lord

   Oth. I had forgot thee: oh come in aemilia.
Soft, by and by, let me the Curtaines draw.
Where art thou? What's the matter with thee now?
Enter aemilia.

Aemil. Oh my good Lord, yonders foule Murthers done

   Oth. What? now?
Aemil. But now, my Lord

   Oth. It is the very error of the Moone,
She comes more neerer Earth then she was wont,
And makes men mad.
Aemil. Cassio, my Lord, hath kill'd
A young Venetian, call'd Rodorigo

   Oth. Rodorigo kill'd? and Cassio kill'd?
Aemil. No, Cassio is not kill'd

   Oth. Not Cassio kill'd? Then Murther's out of tune,
And sweet Reuenge growes harsh

Des. O falsely, falsely murder'd.
Aemil. Alas! what cry is that?
  Oth. That? What?
Aemil. Out, and alas, that was my Ladies voice.
Helpe, helpe hoa, helpe. Oh Ladie speake againe,
Sweet Desdemona, oh sweet Mistris, speake

  Des. A guiltlesse death, I dye.
Aemil. Oh who hath done this deed?
  Des. No body: I my selfe, farewell:
Commend me to my kinde Lord: oh farewell

  Oth. Why, how should she be murdred?
Aemil. Alas: who knowes?
  Oth. You heare her say her selfe, it was not I.
Aemil. She said so: I must needs report the truth

  Oth. She's like a Liar gone to burning hell,
'Twas I that kill'd her.
Aemil. Oh the more Angell she, and you the blacker
Diuell

  Oth. She turn'd to folly: and she was a whore.
Aemil. Thou do'st bely her, and thou art a diuell

  Oth. She was false as water.
Aemil. Thou art rash as fire, to say
That she was false. Oh she was heauenly true

  Oth. Cassio did top her: Ask thy husband else.
O, I were damn'd beneath all depth in hell:
But that I did proceed vpon iust grounds
To this extremity. Thy Husband knew it all.
Aemil. My Husband?
  Oth. Thy Husband.
Aemil. That she was false to Wedlocke?
  Oth. I, with Cassio: had she bin true,
If Heauen would make me such another world,
Of one entyre and perfect Chrysolite,
I'ld not haue sold her for it.
Aemil. My Husband?

Oth. I, 'twas he that told me on her first,
An honest man he is, and hates the slime
That stickes on filthy deeds.
Aemil. My Husband?
 Oth. What needs this itterance, Woman?
I say, thy Husband.
Aemil. Oh Mistris,
Villany hath made mockes with loue:
My Husband say she was false?
 Oth. He, Woman;
I say thy Husband: Do'st vnderstand the word?
My Friend, thy Husband; honest, honest Iago.
Aemil. If he say so, may his pernicious Soule
Rot halfe a graine a day: he lyes to'th' heart,
She was too fond of her most filthy Bargaine

 Oth. Hah?
Aemil. Do thy worst:
This deede of thine is no more worthy Heauen,
Then thou was't worthy her

 Oth. Peace, you were best.
Aemil. Thou hast not halfe that powre to do me harm,
As I haue to be hurt. Oh Gull, oh dolt,
As ignorant as durt: thou hast done a deed
(I care not for thy Sword) Ile make thee known,
Though I lost twenty liues. Helpe, helpe, hoa, helpe:
The Moore hath kill'd my Mistris. Murther, murther.
Enter Montano, Gratiano, and Iago.

 Mon. What is the matter? How now Generall?
Aemil. Oh, are you come, Iago: you haue done well,
That men must lay their Murthers on your necke

 Gra. What is the matter?
Aemil. Disproue this Villaine, if thou bee'st a man:
He sayes, thou told'st him that his wife was false:
I know thou did'st not: thou'rt not such a Villain.
Speake, for my heart is full

Iago. I told him what I thought,
And told no more
Then what he found himselfe was apt, and true.
Aemil. But did you euer tell him,
She was false?
  Iago. I did.
Aemil. You told a Lye an odious damned Lye:
Vpon my Soule, a Lye; a wicked Lye.
Shee false with Cassio?
Did you say with Cassio?
  Iago. With Cassio, Mistris?
Go too, charme your tongue

  Emil. I will not charme my Tongue;
I am bound to speake,
My Mistris heere lyes murthered in her bed

All. Oh Heauens, forefend

Emil. And your reports haue set the Murder on

  Othello. Nay stare not Masters,
It is true indeede

Gra. 'Tis a strange Truth

Mont. O monstrous Acte

  Emil. Villany, villany, villany:
I thinke vpon't, I thinke: I smel't: O Villany:
I thought so then: Ile kill my selfe for greefe.
O villany! villany!
  Iago. What, are you mad?
I charge you get you home

  Emil. Good Gentlemen, let me haue leaue to speake:
'Tis proper I obey him; but not now:
Perchance Iago, I will ne're go home

Oth. Oh, oh, oh

Emil. Nay, lay thee downe, and roare:
For thou hast kill'd the sweetest innocent,
That ere did lift vp eye

Oth. Oh she was fowle!
I scarse did know you Vnkle, there lies your Neece,
Whose breath (indeed) these hands haue newly stopp'd:
I know this acte shewes horrible and grim

Gra. Poore Desdemon:
I am glad thy Father's dead,
Thy Match was mortall to him: and pure greefe
Shore his old thred in twaine. Did he liue now,
This sight would make him do a desperate turne:
Yea, curse his better Angell from his side,
And fall to Reprobance

Oth. 'Tis pittifull: but yet Iago knowes
That she with Cassio, hath the Act of shame
A thousand times committed. Cassio confest it,
And she did gratifie his amorous workes
With that Recognizance and pledge of Loue
Which I first gaue her: I saw it in his hand:
It was a Handkerchiefe, an Antique Token
My Father gaue my Mother

Emil. Oh Heauen! oh heauenly Powres!
Iago. Come, hold your peace

Emil. 'Twill out, 'twill out. I peace?
No, I will speake as liberall as the North;
Let Heauen, and Men, and Diuels, let them all,
All, all, crie shame against me, yet Ile speake

Iago. Be wise, and get you home

Emil. I will not

Gra. Fye, your Sword vpon a Woman

Emil. Oh thou dull Moore,
That Handkerchiefe thou speak'st of

I found by Fortune, and did giue my Husband:
For often, with a solemne earnestnesse,
(More then indeed belong'd to such a Trifle)
He begg'd of me, to steale't

Iago. Villanous Whore

  Emil. She giue it Cassio? No, alas I found it,
And I did giu't my Husband

Iago. Filth, thou lyest

  Emil. By Heauen I do not, I do not Gentlemen:
Oh murd'rous Coxcombe, what should such a Foole
Do with so good a wife?
  Oth. Are there no stones in Heauen,
But what serues for the Thunder?
Precious Villaine

  Gra. The woman falles:
Sure he hath kill'd his Wife

Emil. I, I: oh lay me by my Mistris side

Gra. Hee's gone, but his wife's kill'd

  Mon. 'Tis a notorious Villain: take you this weapon
Which I haue recouer'd from the Moore:
Come guard the doore without, let him not passe,
But kill him rather. Ile after that same villaine,
For 'tis a damned Slaue.
Enter.

  Oth. I am not valiant neither:
But euery Punie whipster gets my Sword.
But why should Honor out-liue Honesty?
Let it go all.
Aemil. What did thy Song boad Lady?
Hearke, canst thou heare me? I will play the Swan,
And dye in Musicke: Willough, Willough, Willough.
Moore, she was chaste: She lou'd thee, cruell Moore,

So come my Soule to blisse, as I speake true:
So speaking as I thinke, alas, I dye

   Oth. I haue another weapon in this Chamber,
It was a Sword of Spaine, the Ice brookes temper:
Oh heere it is: Vnkle I must come forth

   Gra. If thou attempt it, it will cost thee deere;
Thou hast no weapon, and perforce must suffer

   Oth. Looke in vpon me then, and speake with me,
Or naked as I am I will assault thee

   Gra. What is the matter?
   Othel. Behold, I haue a weapon:
A better neuer did it selfe sustaine
Vpon a Soldiers Thigh. I haue seene the day,
That with this little Arme, and this good Sword,
I haue made my way through more impediments
Then twenty times your stop. But (oh vaine boast)
Who can controll his Fate? 'Tis not so now.
Be not affraid, though you do see me weapon'd:
Heere is my iournies end, heere is my butt
And verie Sea-marke of my vtmost Saile.
Do you go backe dismaid? 'Tis a lost feare:
Man but a Rush against Othello's brest,
And he retires. Where should Othello go?
Now: how dost thou looke now? Oh ill-Starr'd wench,
Pale as thy Smocke: when we shall meete at compt,
This looke of thine will hurle my Soule from Heauen,
And Fiends will snatch at it. Cold, cold, my Girle?
Euen like thy Chastity. O cursed, cursed Slaue!
Whip me ye Diuels,
From the possession of this Heauenly sight:
Blow me about in windes, roast me in Sulphure,
Wash me in steepe-downe gulfes of Liquid fire.
Oh Desdemon! dead Desdemon: dead. Oh, oh!
Enter Lodouico, Cassio, Montano, and Iago, with Officers.

   Lod. Where is this rash, and most vnfortunate man?
   Oth. That's he that was Othello: heere I am

Lod. Where is that Viper?
Bring the Villaine forth

Oth. I look down towards his feet; but that's a Fable,
If that thou bee'st a Diuell, I cannot kill thee

Lod. Wrench his Sword from him

Iago. I bleed Sir, but not kill'd

Othel. I am not sorry neither, Il'd haue thee liue:
For in my sense, 'tis happinesse to die

Lod. Oh thou Othello, that was once so good,
Falne in the practise of a cursed Slaue,
What shall be saide to thee

Oth. Why any thing:
An honourable Murderer, if you will:
For nought I did in hate, but all in Honour

Lod. This wretch hath part confest his Villany:
Did you and he consent in Cassio's death

Oth. I

Cas. Deere Generall, I neuer gaue you cause

Oth. I do beleeue it, and I aske your pardon:
Will you, I pray, demand that demy-Diuell,
Why he hath thus ensnar'd my Soule and Body

Iag. Demand me nothing: what you know, you know:
From this time forth, I neuer will speake word

Lod. What? not to pray?
Gra. Torments will ope your lips

Oth. Well, thou dost best

Lod. Sir,
You shall vnderstand what hath befalne,
(Which, as I thinke, you know not) heere is a Letter

Found in the pocket of the slaine Rodorigo,
And heere another, the one of them imports
The death of Cassio, to be vndertooke
By Rodorigo

  Oth. O Villaine!
  Cassio. Most Heathenish, and most grosse

  Lod. Now, heere's another discontented paper
Found in his pocket too: and this it seemes
Rodorigo meant t'haue sent this damned villaine:
But that (belike) Iago in the interim
Came in, and satisfi'd him

  Oth. Oh thou pernitious Caitiffe;
How came you (Cassio) by that Handkerchiefe
That was my wiues?
  Cassio. I found it in my Chamber:
And he himselfe confest it but euen now,
That there he dropt it for a speciall purpose,
Which wrought to his desire

  Othel. O Foole, foole, foole!
  Cassio. There is besides, in Rodorigo's Letter,
How he vpbraides Iago, that he made him
Braue me vpon the Watch: whereon it came
That I was cast: and euen but now he spake
(After long seeming dead) Iago hurt him,
Iago set him on

  Lod. You must forsake this roome, and go with vs:
Your Power, and your Command is taken off,
And Cassio rules in Cyprus. For this Slaue,
If there be any cunning Crueltie,
That can torment him much, and hold him long,
It shall be his. You shall close Prisoner rest,
Till that the Nature of your fault be knowne
To the Venetian State. Come, bring away

  Oth. Soft you; a word or two before you goe:
I haue done the State some seruice, and they know't:

No more of that. I pray you in your Letters,
When you shall these vnluckie deeds relate,
Speake of me, as I am. Nothing extenuate,
Nor set downe ought in malice.
Then must you speake,
Of one that lou'd not wisely, but too well:
Of one, not easily Iealious, but being wrought,
Perplexed in the extreame: Of one, whose hand
(Like the base Iudean) threw a Pearle away
Richer then all his Tribe: Of one, whose subdu'd Eyes,
Albeit vn-vsed to the melting moode,
Drops teares as fast as the Arabian Trees
Their Medicinable gumme. Set you downe this:
And say besides, that in Aleppo once,
Where a malignant, and a Turbond-Turke
Beate a Venetian, and traduc'd the State,
I tooke by th' throat the circumcised Dogge,
And smoate him, thus

Lod. Oh bloody period

Gra. All that is spoke, is marr'd

   Oth. I kist thee, ere I kill'd thee: No way but this,
Killing my selfe, to dye vpon a kisse.

Dyes

   Cas. This did I feare, but thought he had no weapon:
For he was great of heart

   Lod. Oh Sparton Dogge:
More fell then Anguish, Hunger, or the Sea:
Looke on the Tragicke Loading of this bed:
This is thy worke:
The Obiect poysons Sight,
Let it be hid. Gratiano, keepe the house,
And seize vpon the Fortunes of the Moore,
For they succeede on you. To you, Lord Gouernor,
Remaines the Censure of this hellish villaine:
The Time, the Place, the Torture, oh inforce it:

My selfe will straight aboord, and to the State,
This heauie Act, with heauie heart relate.

Exeunt.

FINIS.

The Names of the Actors.

Othello, the Moore.
Brabantio, Father to Desdemona.
Cassio, an Honourable Lieutenant.
Iago, a Villaine.
Rodorigo, a gull'd Gentleman.
Duke of Venice.
Senators.
Montano, Gouernour of Cyprus.
Gentlemen of Cyprus.
Lodouico, and Gratiano, two Noble Venetians.
Saylors.
Clowne.
Desdemona, Wife to Othello.
Aemilia, Wife to Iago.
Bianca, a Curtezan.

THE TRAGEDIE OF Othello, the Moore of Venice.

THE TRAGEDIE OF OTHELLO, THE MOORE OF VENICE

By William Shakespeare

Actus Primus. Scoena Prima.

Enter Rodorigo, and Iago.

Rodorigo. Neuer tell me, I take it much vnkindly
That thou (Iago) who hast had my purse,
As if y strings were thine, should'st know of this

Ia. But you'l not heare me. If euer I did dream
Of such a matter, abhorre me

Rodo. Thou told'st me,
Thou did'st hold him in thy hate

Iago. Despise me
If I do not. Three Great-ones of the Cittie,
(In personall suite to make me his Lieutenant)
Off-capt to him: and by the faith of man
I know my price, I am worth no worsse a place.
But he (as louing his owne pride, and purposes)
Euades them, with a bumbast Circumstance,
Horribly stufft with Epithites of warre,
Non-suites my Mediators. For certes, saies he,
I haue already chose my Officer. And what was he?
For-sooth, a great Arithmatician,
One Michaell Cassio, a Florentine,
(A Fellow almost damn'd in a faire Wife)
That neuer set a Squadron in the Field,
Nor the deuision of a Battaile knowes
More then a Spinster. Vnlesse the Bookish Theoricke:
Wherein the Tongued Consuls can propose
As Masterly as he. Meere pratle (without practise)
Is all his Souldiership. But he (Sir) had th' election;
And I (of whom his eies had seene the proofe
At Rhodes, at Ciprus, and on others grounds
Christen'd, and Heathen) must be be-leed, and calm'd
By Debitor, and Creditor. This Counter-caster,
He (in good time) must his Lieutenant be,
And I (blesse the marke) his Mooreships Auntient

Rod. By heauen, I rather would haue bin his hangman

Iago. Why, there's no remedie.
'Tis the cursse of Seruice;
Preferment goes by Letter, and affection,
And not by old gradation, where each second
Stood Heire to'th' first. Now Sir, be iudge your selfe,
Whether I in any iust terme am Affin'd
To loue the Moore?
Rod. I would not follow him then

Iago. O Sir content you.
I follow him, to serue my turne vpon him.
We cannot all be Masters, nor all Masters
Cannot be truely follow'd. You shall marke
Many a dutious and knee-crooking knaue;
That (doting on his owne obsequious bondage)
Weares out his time, much like his Masters Asse,
For naught but Prouender, & when he's old Casheer'd.
Whip me such honest knaues. Others there are
Who trym'd in Formes, and visages of Dutie,
Keepe yet their hearts attending on themselues,
And throwing but showes of Seruice on their Lords
Doe well thriue by them.
And when they haue lin'd their Coates
Doe themselues Homage.
These Fellowes haue some soule,
And such a one do I professe my selfe. For (Sir)
It is as sure as you are Rodorigo,
Were I the Moore, I would not be Iago:
In following him, I follow but my selfe.
Heauen is my Iudge, not I for loue and dutie,
But seeming so, for my peculiar end:
For when my outward Action doth demonstrate
The natiue act, and figure of my heart
In Complement externe, 'tis not long after
But I will weare my heart vpon my sleeue
For Dawes to pecke at; I am not what I am

Rod. What a fall Fortune do's the Thicks-lips owe
If he can carry't thus?

Iago. Call vp her Father:
Rowse him, make after him, poyson his delight,
Proclaime him in the Streets. Incense her kinsmen,
And though he in a fertile Clymate dwell,
Plague him with Flies: though that his Ioy be Ioy,
Yet throw such chances of vexation on't,
As it may loose some colour

Rodo. Heere is her Fathers house, Ile call aloud

Iago. Doe, with like timerous accent, and dire yell,
As when (by Night and Negligence) the Fire
Is spied in populus Citties

Rodo. What hoa: Brabantio, Signior Brabantio, hoa

Iago. Awake: what hoa, Brabantio: Theeues, Theeues.
Looke to your house, your daughter, and your Bags,
Theeues, Theeues

Bra. Aboue. What is the reason of this terrible
Summons? What is the matter there?
Rodo. Signior is all your Familie within?
Iago. Are your Doores lock'd?
Bra. Why? Wherefore ask you this?
Iago. Sir, y'are rob'd, for shame put on your Gowne,
Your heart is burst, you haue lost halfe your soule
Euen now, now, very now, an old blacke Ram
Is tupping your white Ewe. Arise, arise,
Awake the snorting Cittizens with the Bell,
Or else the deuill will make a Grand-sire of you.
Arise I say

Bra. What, haue you lost your wits?
Rod. Most reuerend Signior, do you know my voice?
Bra. Not I: what are you?
Rod. My name is Rodorigo

Bra. The worsser welcome:
I haue charg'd thee not to haunt about my doores:
In honest plainenesse thou hast heard me say,
My Daughter is not for thee. And now in madnesse

(Being full of Supper, and distempring draughtes)
Vpon malitious knauerie, dost thou come
To start my quiet

Rod. Sir, Sir, Sir

  Bra. But thou must needs be sure,
My spirits and my place haue in their power
To make this bitter to thee

Rodo. Patience good Sir

  Bra. What tell'st thou me of Robbing?
This is Venice: my house is not a Grange

  Rodo. Most graue Brabantio,
In simple and pure soule, I come to you

Ia. Sir: you are one of those that will not serue God, if the deuill bid you.
Because we come to do you seruice, and you thinke we are Ruffians, you'le
haue your Daughter couer'd with a Barbary horse, you'le haue your
Nephewes neigh to you, you'le haue Coursers for Cozens: and Gennets for
Germaines

  Bra. What prophane wretch art thou?
  Ia. I am one Sir, that comes to tell you, your Daughter
and the Moore, are making the Beast with two backs

Bra. Thou art a Villaine

Iago. You are a Senator

Bra. This thou shalt answere. I know thee Rodorigo

  Rod. Sir, I will answere any thing. But I beseech you
If't be your pleasure, and most wise consent,
(As partly I find it is) that your faire Daughter,
At this odde Euen and dull watch o'th' night
Transported with no worse nor better guard,
But with a knaue of common hire, a Gundelier,
To the grosse claspes of a Lasciuious Moore:
If this be knowne to you, and your Allowance,

We then haue done you bold, and saucie wrongs.
But if you know not this, my Manners tell me,
We haue your wrong rebuke. Do not beleeue
That from the sence of all Ciuilitie,
I thus would play and trifle with your Reuerence.
Your Daughter (if you haue not giuen her leaue)
I say againe, hath made a grosse reuolt,
Tying her Dutie, Beautie, Wit, and Fortunes
In an extrauagant, and wheeling Stranger,
Of here, and euery where: straight satisfie your selfe.
If she be in her Chamber, or your house,
Let loose on me the Iustice of the State
For thus deluding you

  Bra. Strike on the Tinder, hoa:
Giue me a Taper: call vp all my people,
This Accident is not vnlike my dreame,
Beleefe of it oppresses me alreadie.
Light, I say, light.
Enter.

  Iag. Farewell: for I must leaue you.
It seemes not meete, nor wholesome to my place
To be producted, (as if I stay, I shall,)
Against the Moore. For I do know the State,
(How euer this may gall him with some checke)
Cannot with safetie cast-him. For he's embark'd
With such loud reason to the Cyprus Warres,
(Which euen now stands in Act) that for their soules
Another of his Fadome, they haue none,
To lead their Businesse. In which regard,
Though I do hate him as I do hell paines,
Yet, for necessitie of present life,
I must show out a Flag, and signe of Loue,
(Which is indeed but signe) that you shal surely find him
Lead to the Sagitary the raised Search:
And there will I be with him. So farewell.

Enter.

Enter Brabantio, with Seruants and Torches.

Bra. It is too true an euill. Gone she is,
And what's to come of my despised time,
Is naught but bitternesse. Now Rodorigo,
Where didst thou see her? (Oh vnhappie Girle)
With the Moore saist thou? (Who would be a Father?)
How didst thou know 'twas she? (Oh she deceaues me
Past thought:) what said she to you? Get moe Tapers.
Raise all my Kindred. Are they married thinke you?
  Rodo. Truely I thinke they are

  Bra. Oh Heauen: how got she out?
Oh treason of the blood.
Fathers, from hence trust not your Daughters minds
By what you see them act. Is there not Charmes,
By which the propertie of Youth, and Maidhood
May be abus'd? Haue you not read Rodorigo,
Of some such thing?
  Rod. Yes Sir: I haue indeed

  Bra. Call vp my Brother: oh would you had had her.
Some one way, some another. Doe you know
Where we may apprehend her, and the Moore?
  Rod. I thinke I can discouer him, if you please
To get good Guard, and go along with me

  Bra. Pray you lead on. At euery house Ile call,
(I may command at most) get Weapons (hoa)
And raise some speciall Officers of might:
On good Rodorigo, I will deserue your paines.

Exeunt.

Scena Secunda.

Enter Othello, Iago, Attendants, with Torches.

  Ia. Though in the trade of Warre I haue slaine men,
Yet do I hold it very stuffe o'th' conscience
To do no contriu'd Murder: I lacke Iniquitie
Sometime to do me seruice. Nine, or ten times
I had thought t'haue yerk'd him here vnder the Ribbes

Othello. 'Tis better as it is

  Iago. Nay but he prated,
And spoke such scuruy, and prouoking termes
Against your Honor, that with the little godlinesse I haue
I did full hard forbeare him. But I pray you Sir,
Are you fast married? Be assur'd of this,
That the Magnifico is much belou'd,
And hath in his effect a voice potentiall
As double as the Dukes: He will diuorce you.
Or put vpon you, what restraint or greeuance,
The Law (with all his might, to enforce it on)
Will giue him Cable

  Othel. Let him do his spight;
My Seruices, which I haue done the Signorie
Shall out-tongue his Complaints. 'Tis yet to know,
Which when I know, that boasting is an Honour,
I shall promulgate. I fetch my life and being,
From Men of Royall Seige. And my demerites
May speake (vnbonnetted) to as proud a Fortune
As this that I haue reach'd. For know Iago,
But that I loue the gentle Desdemona,
I would not my vnhoused free condition
Put into Circumscription, and Confine,
For the Seas worth. But looke, what Lights come yond?

Enter Cassio, with Torches.

  Iago. Those are the raised Father, and his Friends:
You were best go in

  Othel. Not I: I must be found.
My Parts, my Title, and my perfect Soule
Shall manifest me rightly. Is it they?
  Iago. By Ianus, I thinke no

  Othel. The Seruants of the Dukes?
And my Lieutenant?
The goodnesse of the Night vpon you (Friends)
What is the Newes?

Cassio. The Duke do's greet you (Generall)
And he requires your haste, Post-haste appearance,
Euen on the instant

  Othello. What is the matter, thinke you?
  Cassio. Something from Cyprus, as I may diuine:
It is a businesse of some heate. The Gallies
Haue sent a dozen sequent Messengers
This very night, at one anothers heeles:
And many of the Consuls, rais'd and met,
Are at the Dukes already. You haue bin hotly call'd for,
When being not at your Lodging to be found,
The Senate hath sent about three seuerall Quests,
To search you out

  Othel. 'Tis well I am found by you:
I will but spend a word here in the house,
And goe with you

  Cassio. Aunciant, what makes he heere?
  Iago. Faith, he to night hath boarded a Land Carract,
If it proue lawfull prize, he's made for euer

Cassio. I do not vnderstand

Iago. He's married

  Cassio. To who?
  Iago. Marry to- Come Captaine, will you go?
  Othel. Haue with you

Cassio. Here comes another Troope to seeke for you.

Enter Brabantio, Rodorigo, with Officers, and Torches.

  Iago. It is Brabantio: Generall be aduis'd,
He comes to bad intent

Othello. Holla, stand there

Rodo. Signior, it is the Moore

Bra. Downe with him, Theefe

Iago. You, Rodorigo? Come Sir, I am for you

Othe. Keepe vp your bright Swords, for the dew will rust them. Good
Signior, you shall more command with yeares, then with your Weapons

   Bra. Oh thou foule Theefe,
Where hast thou stow'd my Daughter?
Damn'd as thou art, thou hast enchaunted her
For Ile referre me to all things of sense,
(If she in Chaines of Magick were not bound)
Whether a Maid, so tender, Faire, and Happie,
So opposite to Marriage, that she shun'd
The wealthy curled Deareling of our Nation,
Would euer haue (t' encurre a generall mocke)
Run from her Guardage to the sootie bosome,
Of such a thing as thou: to feare, not to delight?
Iudge me the world, if 'tis not grosse in sense,
That thou hast practis'd on her with foule Charmes,
Abus'd her delicate Youth, with Drugs or Minerals,
That weakens Motion. Ile haue't disputed on,
'Tis probable, and palpable to thinking;
I therefore apprehend and do attach thee,
For an abuser of the World, a practiser
Of Arts inhibited, and out of warrant;
Lay hold vpon him, if he do resist
Subdue him, at his perill

   Othe. Hold your hands
Both you of my inclining, and the rest.
Were it my Cue to fight, I should haue knowne it
Without a Prompter. Whether will you that I goe
To answere this your charge?
   Bra. To Prison, till fit time
Of Law, and course of direct Session
Call thee to answer

   Othe. What if I do obey?
How may the Duke be therewith satisfi'd,
Whose Messengers are heere about my side,
Vpon some present businesse of the State,
To bring me to him

Officer. 'Tis true most worthy Signior,
The Dukes in Counsell, and your Noble selfe,
I am sure is sent for

Bra. How? The Duke in Counsell?
In this time of the night? Bring him away;
Mine's not an idle Cause. The Duke himselfe,
Or any of my Brothers of the State,
Cannot but feele this wrong, as 'twere their owne:
For if such Actions may haue passage free,
Bond-slaues, and Pagans shall our Statesmen be.

Exeunt.

Scaena Tertia.

Enter Duke, Senators, and Officers.

Duke. There's no composition in this Newes,
That giues them Credite

1.Sen. Indeed, they are disproportioned;
My Letters say, a Hundred and seuen Gallies

Duke. And mine a Hundred fortie

2.Sena. And mine two Hundred:
But though they iumpe not on a iust accompt,
(As in these Cases where the ayme reports,
'Tis oft with difference) yet do they all confirme
A Turkish Fleete, and bearing vp to Cyprus

Duke. Nay, it is possible enough to iudgement:
I do not so secure me in the Error,
But the maine Article I do approue
In fearefull sense

Saylor within. What hoa, what hoa, what hoa.

Enter Saylor.

Officer. A Messenger from the Gallies

Duke. Now? What's the businesse?

Sailor. The Turkish Preparation makes for Rhodes,
So was I bid report here to the State,
By Signior Angelo

Duke. How say you by this change?

1.Sen. This cannot be
By no assay of reason. 'Tis a Pageant
To keepe vs in false gaze, when we consider
Th' importancie of Cyprus to the Turke;
And let our selues againe but vnderstand,
That as it more concernes the Turke then Rhodes,
So may he with more facile question beare it,
For that it stands not in such Warrelike brace,
But altogether lackes th' abilities
That Rhodes is dress'd in. If we make thought of this,
We must not thinke the Turke is so vnskillfull,
To leaue that latest, which concernes him first,
Neglecting an attempt of ease, and gaine
To wake, and wage a danger profitlesse

Duke. Nay, in all confidence he's not for Rhodes

Officer. Here is more Newes.

Enter a Messenger.

Messen. The Ottamites, Reueren'd, and Gracious,
Steering with due course toward the Ile of Rhodes,
Haue there inioynted them with an after Fleete

1.Sen. I, so I thought: how many, as you guesse?

Mess. Of thirtie Saile: and now they do re-stem
Their backward course, bearing with frank appearance
Their purposes toward Cyprus. Signior Montano,
Your trustie and most Valiant Seruitour,
With his free dutie, recommends you thus,
And prayes you to beleeue him

Duke. 'Tis certaine then for Cyprus:
Marcus Luccicos is not he in Towne?

1.Sen. He's now in Florence

Duke. Write from vs,
To him, Post, Post-haste, dispatch

1.Sen. Here comes Brabantio, and the Valiant Moore.

Enter Brabantio, Othello, Cassio, Iago, Rodorigo, and Officers.

  Duke. Valiant Othello, we must straight employ you,
Against the generall Enemy Ottoman.
I did not see you: welcome gentle Signior,
We lack't your Counsaile, and your helpe to night

  Bra. So did I yours: Good your Grace pardon me.
Neither my place, nor ought I heard of businesse
Hath rais'd me from my bed; nor doth the generall care
Take hold on me. For my perticular griefe
Is of so flood-gate, and ore-bearing Nature,
That it engluts, and swallowes other sorrowes,
And it is still it selfe

  Duke. Why? What's the matter?
  Bra. My Daughter: oh my Daughter!
  Sen. Dead?
  Bra. I, to me.
She is abus'd, stolne from me, and corrupted
By Spels, and Medicines, bought of Mountebanks;
For Nature, so prepostrously to erre,
(Being not deficient, blind, or lame of sense,)
Sans witch-craft could not

  Duke. Who ere he be, that in this foule proceeding
Hath thus beguil'd your Daughter of her selfe,
And you of her; the bloodie Booke of Law,
You shall your selfe read, in the bitter letter,
After your owne sense: yea, though our proper Son
Stood in your Action

  Bra. Humbly I thanke your Grace,
Here is the man; this Moore, whom now it seemes
Your speciall Mandate, for the State affaires
Hath hither brought

All. We are verie sorry for't

  Duke. What in your owne part, can you say to this?
Bra. Nothing, but this is so

  Othe. Most Potent, Graue, and Reueren'd Signiors,
My very Noble, and approu'd good Masters;
That I haue tane away this old mans Daughter,
It is most true: true I haue married her;
The verie head, and front of my offending,
Hath this extent; no more. Rude am I, in my speech,
And little bless'd with the soft phrase of Peace;
For since these Armes of mine, had seuen yeares pith,
Till now, some nine Moones wasted, they haue vs'd
Their deerest action, in the Tented Field:
And little of this great world can I speake,
More then pertaines to Feats of Broiles, and Battaile,
And therefore little shall I grace my cause,
In speaking for my selfe. Yet, (by your gratious patience)
I will a round vn-varnish'd Tale deliuer,
Of my whole course of Loue.
What Drugges, what Charmes,
What Coniuration, and what mighty Magicke,
(For such proceeding I am charg'd withall)
I won his Daughter

  Bra. A Maiden, neuer bold:
Of Spirit so still, and quiet, that her Motion
Blush'd at her selfe, and she, in spight of Nature,
Of Yeares, of Country, Credite, euery thing
To fall in Loue, with what she fear'd to looke on;
It is a iudgement main'd, and most imperfect.
That will confesse Perfection so could erre
Against all rules of Nature, and must be driuen
To find out practises of cunning hell
Why this should be. I therefore vouch againe,
That with some Mixtures, powrefull o're the blood,
Or with some Dram, (coniur'd to this effect)
He wrought vpon her.
To vouch this, is no proofe,
Without more wider, and more ouer Test

Then these thin habits, and poore likely-hoods
Of moderne seeming, do prefer against him

   Sen. But Othello, speake,
Did you, by indirect, and forced courses
Subdue, and poyson this yong Maides affections?
Or came it by request, and such faire question
As soule, to soule affordeth?
   Othel. I do beseech you,
Send for the Lady to the Sagitary,
And let her speake of me before her Father;
If you do finde me foule, in her report,
The Trust, the Office, I do hold of you,
Not onely take away, but let your Sentence
Euen fall vpon my life

Duke. Fetch Desdemona hither

   Othe. Aunciant, conduct them:
You best know the place.
And tell she come, as truely as to heauen,
I do confesse the vices of my blood,
So iustly to your Graue eares, Ile present
How I did thriue in this faire Ladies loue,
And she in mine

Duke. Say it Othello

   Othe. Her Father lou'd me, oft inuited me:
Still question'd me the Storie of my life,
From yeare to yeare: the Battaile, Sieges, Fortune,
That I haue past.
I ran it through, euen from my boyish daies,
Toth' very moment that he bad me tell it.
Wherein I spoke of most disastrous chances:
Of mouing Accidents by Flood and Field,
Of haire-breadth scapes i'th' imminent deadly breach;
Of being taken by the Insolent Foe,
And sold to slauery. Of my redemption thence,
And portance in my Trauellours historie.
Wherein of Antars vast, and Desarts idle,

Rough Quarries, Rocks, Hills, whose head touch heauen,
It was my hint to speake. Such was my Processe,
And of the Canibals that each others eate,
The Antropophague, and men whose heads
Grew beneath their shoulders. These things to heare,
Would Desdemona seriously incline:
But still the house Affaires would draw her hence:
Which euer as she could with haste dispatch,
She'l'd come againe, and with a greedie eare
Deuoure vp my discourse. Which I obseruing,
Tooke once a pliant houre, and found good meanes
To draw from her a prayer of earnest heart,
That I would all my Pilgrimage dilate,
Whereof by parcels she had something heard,
But not instinctiuely: I did consent,
And often did beguile her of her teares,
When I did speake of some distressefull stroke
That my youth suffer'd: My Storie being done,
She gaue me for my paines a world of kisses:
She swore in faith 'twas strange: 'twas passing strange,
'Twas pittifull: 'twas wondrous pittifull.
She wish'd she had not heard it, yet she wish'd
That Heauen had made her such a man. She thank'd me,
And bad me, if I had a Friend that lou'd her,
I should but teach him how to tell my Story,
And that would wooe her. Vpon this hint I spake,
She lou'd me for the dangers I had past,
And I lou'd her, that she did pitty them.
This onely is the witch-craft I haue vs'd.
Here comes the Ladie: Let her witnesse it.

Enter Desdemona, Iago, Attendants.

  Duke. I thinke this tale would win my Daughter too,
Good Brabantio, take vp this mangled matter at the best:
Men do their broken Weapons rather vse,
Then their bare hands

  Bra. I pray you heare her speake?
If she confesse that she was halfe the wooer,
Destruction on my head, if my bad blame

Light on the man. Come hither gentle Mistris,
Do you perceiue in all this Noble Companie,
Where most you owe obedience?
  Des. My Noble Father,
I do perceiue heere a diuided dutie.
To you I am bound for life, and education:
My life and education both do learne me,
How to respect you. You are the Lord of duty,
I am hitherto your Daughter. But heere's my Husband;
And so much dutie, as my Mother shew'd
To you, preferring you before her Father:
So much I challenge, that I may professe
Due to the Moore my Lord

  Bra. God be with you: I haue done.
Please it your Grace, on to the State Affaires;
I had rather to adopt a Child, then get it.
Come hither Moore;
I here do giue thee that with all my heart,
Which but thou hast already, with all my heart
I would keepe from thee. For your sake (Iewell)
I am glad at soule, I haue no other Child,
For thy escape would teach me Tirranie
To hang clogges on them. I haue done my Lord

  Duke. Let me speake like your selfe:
And lay a Sentence,
Which as a grise, or step may helpe these Louers.
When remedies are past, the griefes are ended
By seeing the worst, which late on hopes depended.
To mourne a Mischeefe that is past and gon,
Is the next way to draw new mischiefe on.
What cannot be preseru'd, when Fortune takes:
Patience, her Iniury a mock'ry makes.
The rob'd that smiles, steales something from the Thiefe,
He robs himselfe, that spends a bootelesse griefe

  Bra. So let the Turke of Cyprus vs beguile,
We loose it not so long as we can smile:
He beares the Sentence well, that nothing beares,
But the free comfort which from thence he heares.

But he beares both the Sentence, and the sorrow,
That to pay griefe, must of poore Patience borrow.
These Sentences, to Sugar, or to Gall,
Being strong on both sides, are Equiuocall.
But words are words, I neuer yet did heare:
That the bruized heart was pierc'd through the eares.
I humbly beseech you proceed to th' Affaires of State

Duke. The Turke with a most mighty Preparation makes for Cyprus:
Othello, the Fortitude of the place is best knowne to you. And though we
haue there a Substitute of most allowed sufficiencie; yet opinion, a more
soueraigne Mistris of Effects, throwes a more safer voice on you: you must
therefore be content to slubber the glosse of your new Fortunes, with this
more stubborne, and boystrous expedition

   Othe. The Tirant Custome, most Graue Senators,
Hath made the flinty and Steele Coach of Warre
My thrice-driuen bed of Downe. I do agnize
A Naturall and prompt Alacratie,
I finde in hardnesse: and do vndertake
This present Warres against the Ottamites.
Most humbly therefore bending to your State,
I craue fit disposition for my Wife,
Due reference of Place, and Exhibition,
With such Accomodation and besort
As leuels with her breeding

   Duke. Why at her Fathers?
  Bra. I will not haue it so

Othe. Nor I

   Des. Nor would I there recide,
To put my Father in impatient thoughts
By being in his eye. Most Gracious Duke,
To my vnfolding, lend your prosperous eare,
And let me finde a Charter in your voice
T' assist my simplenesse

   Duke. What would you Desdemona?
  Des. That I loue the Moore, to liue with him,

My downe-right violence, and storme of Fortunes,
May trumpet to the world. My heart's subdu'd
Euen to the very quality of my Lord;
I saw Othello's visage in his mind,
And to his Honours and his valiant parts,
Did I my soule and Fortunes consecrate.
So that (deere Lords) if I be left behind
A Moth of Peace, and he go to the Warre,
The Rites for why I loue him, are bereft me:
And I a heauie interim shall support
By his deere absence. Let me go with him

  Othe. Let her haue your voice.
Vouch with me Heauen, I therefore beg it not
To please the pallate of my Appetite:
Nor to comply with heat the yong affects
In my defunct, and proper satisfaction.
But to be free, and bounteous to her minde:
And Heauen defend your good soules, that you thinke
I will your serious and great businesse scant
When she is with me. No, when light wing'd Toyes
Of feather'd Cupid, seele with wanton dulnesse
My speculatiue, and offic'd Instrument:
That my Disports corrupt, and taint my businesse:
Let House-wiues make a Skillet of my Helme,
And all indigne, and base aduersities,
Make head against my Estimation

  Duke. Be it as you shall priuately determine,
Either for her stay, or going: th' Affaire cries hast:
And speed must answer it

Sen. You must away to night

Othe. With all my heart

  Duke. At nine i'th' morning, here wee'l meete againe.
Othello, leaue some Officer behind
And he shall our Commission bring to you:
And such things else of qualitie and respect
As doth import you

Othe. So please your Grace, my Ancient,
A man he is of honesty and trust:
To his conueyance I assigne my wife,
With what else needfull, your good Grace shall think
To be sent after me

  Duke. Let it be so:
Good night to euery one. And Noble Signior,
If Vertue no delighted Beautie lacke,
Your Son-in-law is farre more Faire then Blacke

Sen. Adieu braue Moore, vse Desdemona well

  Bra. Looke to her (Moore) if thou hast eies to see:
She ha's deceiu'd her Father, and may thee.
Enter.

  Othe. My life vpon her faith. Honest Iago,
My Desdemona must I leaue to thee:
I prythee let thy wife attend on her,
And bring them after in the best aduantage.
Come Desdemona, I haue but an houre
Of Loue, of wordly matter, and direction
To spend with thee. We must obey the time.
Enter.

Rod. Iago

  Iago. What saist thou Noble heart?
  Rod. What will I do, think'st thou?
  Iago. Why go to bed and sleepe

Rod. I will incontinently drowne my selfe

Iago. If thou do'st, I shall neuer loue thee after. Why thou silly
Gentleman? Rod. It is sillynesse to liue, when to liue is torment: and then
haue we a prescription to dye, when death is our Physition

Iago. Oh villanous: I haue look'd vpon the world for foure times seuen
yeares, and since I could distinguish betwixt a Benefit, and an Iniurie: I
neuer found man that knew how to loue himselfe. Ere I would say, I

would drowne my selfe for the loue of a Gynney Hen, I would change my Humanity with a Baboone

    Rod. What should I do? I confesse it is my shame to be so fond, but it is not in my vertue to amend it

Iago. Vertue? A figge, 'tis in our selues that we are thus, or thus. Our Bodies are our Gardens, to the which, our Wills are Gardiners. So that if we will plant Nettels, or sowe Lettice: Set Hisope, and weede vp Time: Supplie it with one gender of Hearbes, or distract it with many: either to haue it sterrill with idlenesse, or manured with Industry, why the power, and Corrigeable authoritie of this lies in our Wills. If the braine of our liues had not one Scale of Reason, to poize another of Sensualitie, the blood, and basenesse of our Natures would conduct vs to most prepostrous Conclusions. But we haue Reason to coole our raging Motions, our carnall Stings, or vnbitted Lusts: whereof I take this, that you call Loue, to be a Sect, or Seyen

Rod. It cannot be

Iago. It is meerly a Lust of the blood, and a permission of the will. Come, be a man: drowne thy selfe? Drown Cats, and blind Puppies. I haue profest me thy Friend, and I confesse me knit to thy deseruing, with Cables of perdurable toughnesse. I could neuer better steed thee then now. Put Money in thy purse: follow thou the Warres, defeate thy fauour, with an vsurp'd Beard. I say put Money in thy purse. It cannot be long that Desdemona should continue her loue to the Moore. Put Money in thy purse: nor he his to her. It was a violent Commencement in her, and thou shalt see an answerable Sequestration, put but Money in thy purse. These Moores are changeable in their wils: fill thy purse with Money. The Food that to him now is as lushious as Locusts, shalbe to him shortly, as bitter as Coloquintida. She must change for youth: when she is sated with his body she will find the errors of her choice. Therefore, put Money in thy purse. If thou wilt needs damne thy selfe, do it a more delicate way then drowning. Make all the Money thou canst: If Sanctimonie, and a fraile vow, betwixt an erring Barbarian, and super-subtle Venetian be not too hard for my wits, and all the Tribe of hell, thou shalt enioy her: therefore make Money: a pox of drowning thy selfe, it is cleane out of the way. Seeke thou rather to be hang'd in Compassing thy ioy, then to be drown'd, and go without her

Rodo. Wilt thou be fast to my hopes, if I depend on the issue? Iago. Thou art sure of me: Go make Money: I haue told thee often, and I re-tell thee againe, and againe, I hate the Moore. My cause is hearted; thine hath no lesse reason. Let vs be coniunctiue in our reuenge, against him. If thou canst Cuckold him, thou dost thy selfe a pleasure, me a sport. There are many Euents in the Wombe of Time, which wilbe deliuered. Trauerse, go, prouide thy Money. We will haue more of this to morrow. Adieu

   Rod. Where shall we meete i'th' morning?
   Iago. At my Lodging

Rod. Ile be with thee betimes

   Iago. Go too, farewell. Do you heare Rodorigo?
   Rod. Ile sell all my Land.
Enter.

   Iago. Thus do I euer make my Foole, my purse:
For I mine owne gain'd knowledge should prophane
If I would time expend with such Snipe,
But for my Sport, and Profit: I hate the Moore,
And it is thought abroad, that 'twixt my sheets
She ha's done my Office. I know not if't be true,
But I, for meere suspition in that kinde,
Will do, as if for Surety. He holds me well,
The better shall my purpose worke on him:
Cassio's a proper man: Let me see now,
To get his Place, and to plume vp my will
In double Knauery. How? How? Let's see.
After some time, to abuse Othello's eares,
That he is too familiar with his wife:
He hath a person, and a smooth dispose
To be suspected: fram'd to make women false.
The Moore is of a free, and open Nature,
That thinkes men honest, that but seeme to be so,
And will as tenderly be lead by'th' Nose
As Asses are:
I hau't: it is engendred: Hell, and Night,
Must bring this monstrous Birth, to the worlds light.

Actus Secundus. Scena Prima.

Enter Montano, and two Gentlemen.

  Mon. What from the Cape, can you discerne at Sea?
  1.Gent. Nothing at all, it is a high wrought Flood:
I cannot 'twixt the Heauen, and the Maine,
Descry a Saile

  Mon. Me thinks, the wind hath spoke aloud at Land,
A fuller blast ne're shooke our Battlements:
If it hath ruffiand so vpon the Sea,
What ribbes of Oake, when Mountaines melt on them,
Can hold the Morties. What shall we heare of this?
  2 A Segregation of the Turkish Fleet:
For do but stand vpon the Foaming Shore,
The chidden Billow seemes to pelt the Clowds,
The winde-shak'd-Surge, with high & monstrous Maine
Seemes to cast water on the burning Beare,
And quench the Guards of th' euer-fixed Pole:
I neuer did like mollestation view
On the enchafed Flood

  Men. If that the Turkish Fleete
Be not enshelter'd, and embay'd, they are drown'd,
It is impossible to beare it out.
Enter a Gentleman.

  3 Newes Laddes: our warres are done:
The desperate Tempest hath so bang'd the Turkes,
That their designement halts. A Noble ship of Venice,
Hath seene a greeuous wracke and sufferance
On most part of their Fleet

  Mon. How? Is this true?
  3 The Ship is heere put in: A Verennessa, Michael Cassio
Lieutenant to the warlike Moore, Othello,
Is come on Shore: the Moore himselfe at Sea,
And is in full Commission heere for Cyprus

  Mon. I am glad on't:
'Tis a worthy Gouernour

3 But this same Cassio, though he speake of comfort,
Touching the Turkish losse, yet he lookes sadly,
And praye the Moore be safe; for they were parted
With fowle and violent Tempest

   Mon. Pray Heauens he be:
For I haue seru'd him, and the man commands
Like a full Soldier. Let's to the Sea-side (hoa)
As well to see the Vessell that's come in,
As to throw-out our eyes for braue Othello,
Euen till we make the Maine, and th' Eriall blew,
An indistinct regard

   Gent. Come, let's do so;
For euery Minute is expectancie
Of more Arriuancie.
Enter Cassio.

   Cassi. Thankes you, the valiant of the warlike Isle,
That so approoue the Moore: Oh let the Heauens
Giue him defence against the Elements,
For I haue lost him on a dangerous Sea

   Mon. Is he well ship'd?
   Cassio. His Barke is stoutly Timber'd, and his Pylot
Of verie expert, and approu'd Allowance;
Therefore my hope's (not surfetted to death)
Stand in bold Cure

Within. A Saile, a Saile, a Saile

   Cassio. What noise?
   Gent. The Towne is empty; on the brow o'th' Sea
Stand rankes of People and they cry, a Saile

Cassio. My hopes do shape him for the Gouernor

   Gent. They do discharge their Shot of Courtesie,
Our Friends, at least

   Cassio. I pray you Sir, go forth,
And giue vs truth who 'tis that is arriu'd

Gent. I shall.
Enter.

  Mon. But good Lieutenant, is your Generall wiu'd?
  Cassio. Most fortunately: he hath atchieu'd a Maid
That paragons description, and wilde Fame:
One that excels the quirkes of Blazoning pens,
And in th' essentiall Vesture of Creation,
Do's tyre the Ingeniuer.
Enter Gentleman.

How now? Who ha's put in?
  Gent. 'Tis one Iago, Auncient to the Generall

  Cassio. Ha's had most fauourable, and happie speed:
Tempests themselues, high Seas, and howling windes,
The gutter'd-Rockes, and Congregated Sands,
Traitors ensteep'd, to enclogge the guiltlesse Keele,
As hauing sence of Beautie, do omit
Their mortall Natures, letting go safely by
The Diuine Desdemona

  Mon. What is she?
  Cassio. She that I spake of:
Our great Captains Captaine,
Left in the conduct of the bold Iago,
Whose footing heere anticipates our thoughts,
A Senights speed. Great Ioue, Othello guard,
And swell his Saile with thine owne powrefull breath,
That he may blesse this Bay with his tall Ship,
Make loues quicke pants in Desdemonaes Armes,
Giue renew'd fire to our extincted Spirits.

Enter Desdemona, Iago, Rodorigo, and Aemilia.

Oh behold,
The Riches of the Ship is come on shore:
You men of Cyprus, let her haue your knees.
Haile to thee Ladie: and the grace of Heauen,
Before, behinde thee, and on euery hand
Enwheele thee round

Des. I thanke you, Valiant Cassio,
What tydings can you tell of my Lord?
  Cas. He is not yet arriu'd, nor know I ought
But that he's well, and will be shortly heere

  Des. Oh, but I feare:
How lost you company?
  Cassio. The great Contention of Sea, and Skies
Parted our fellowship. But hearke, a Saile

Within. A Saile, a Saile

  Gent. They giue this greeting to the Cittadell:
This likewise is a Friend

  Cassio. See for the Newes:
Good Ancient, you are welcome. Welcome Mistris:
Let it not gaule your patience (good Iago)
That I extend my Manners. 'Tis my breeding,
That giues me this bold shew of Curtesie

  Iago. Sir, would she giue you so much of her lippes,
As of her tongue she oft bestowes on me,
You would haue enough

Des. Alas: she ha's no speech

  Iago. Infaith too much:
I finde it still, when I haue leaue to sleepe.
Marry before your Ladyship, I grant,
She puts her tongue a little in her heart,
And chides with thinking

aemil. You haue little cause to say so

  Iago. Come on, come on: you are Pictures out of
doore: Bells in your Parlours: Wilde-Cats in your Kitchens:
Saints in your Iniuries: Diuels being offended:
Players in your Huswiferie, and Huswiues in your
Beds

Des. Oh, fie vpon thee, Slanderer

Iago. Nay, it is true: or else I am a Turke,
You rise to play, and go to bed to worke.
Aemil. You shall not write my praise

Iago. No, let me not

Desde. What would'st write of me, if thou should'st
praise me?
Iago. Oh, gentle Lady, do not put me too't,
For I am nothing, if not Criticall

Des. Come on, assay.
There's one gone to the Harbour?
Iago. I Madam

Des. I am not merry: but I do beguile
The thing I am, by seeming otherwise.
Come, how would'st thou praise me?
Iago. I am about it, but indeed my inuention comes
from my pate, as Birdlyme do's from Freeze, it pluckes
out Braines and all. But my Muse labours, and thus she
is deliuer'd.
If she be faire, and wise: fairenesse, and wit,
The ones for vse, the other vseth it

Des. Well prais'd:
How if she be Blacke and Witty?
Iago. If she be blacke, and thereto haue a wit,
She'le find a white, that shall her blacknesse fit

Des. Worse, and worse.
Aemil. How if Faire, and Foolish?
Iago. She neuer yet was foolish that was faire,
For euen her folly helpt her to an heire

Desde. These are old fond Paradoxes, to make Fooles laugh i'th' Alehouse.
What miserable praise hast thou for her that's Foule, and Foolish

Iago. There's none so foule and foolish thereunto,
But do's foule pranks, which faire, and wise-ones do

Desde. Oh heauy ignorance: thou praisest the worst best. But what praise could'st thou bestow on a deseruing woman indeed? One, that in the authorithy of her merit, did iustly put on the vouch of very malice it selfe

Iago. She that was euer faire, and neuer proud,
Had Tongue at will, and yet was neuer loud:
Neuer lackt Gold, and yet went neuer gay,
Fled from her wish, and yet said now I may.
She that being angred, her reuenge being nie,
Bad her wrong stay, and her displeasure flie:
She that in wisedome neuer was so fraile,
To change the Cods-head for the Salmons taile:
She that could thinke, and neu'r disclose her mind,
See Suitors following, and not looke behind:
She was a wight, (if euer such wightes were)
  Des. To do what?
  Iago. To suckle Fooles, and chronicle small Beere

Desde. Oh most lame and impotent conclusion. Do not learne of him aemillia, though he be thy husband. How say you (Cassio) is he not a most prophane, and liberall Counsailor? Cassio. He speakes home (Madam) you may rellish him more in the Souldier, then in the Scholler

Iago. He takes her by the palme: I, well said, whisper. With as little a web as this, will I ensnare as great a Fly as Cassio. I smile vpon her, do: I will giue thee in thine owne Courtship. You say true, 'tis so indeed. If such tricks as these strip you out of your Lieutenantrie, it had beene better you had not kiss'd your three fingers so oft, which now againe you are most apt to play the Sir, in. Very good: well kiss'd, and excellent Curtsie: 'tis so indeed. Yet againe, your fingers to your lippes? Would they were Cluster-pipes for your sake. The Moore I know his Trumpet

Cassio. 'Tis truely so

Des. Let's meete him, and recieue him

  Cassio. Loe, where he comes.
Enter Othello, and Attendants.

Oth. O, my faire Warriour

Des. My deere Othello

Othe. It giues me wonder great, as my content
To see you heere before me.
Oh my Soules Ioy:
If after euery Tempest, come such Calmes,
May the windes blow, till they haue waken'd death:
And let the labouring Barke climbe hills of Seas
Olympus high: and duck againe as low,
As hell's from Heauen. If it were now to dye,
'Twere now to be most happy. For I feare,
My Soule hath her content so absolute,
That not another comfort like to this,
Succeedes in vnknowne Fate

  Des. The Heauens forbid
But that our Loues
And Comforts should encrease
Euen as our dayes do grow

  Othe. Amen to that (sweet Powers)
I cannot speake enough of this content,
It stoppes me heere: it is too much of ioy.
And this, and this the greatest discords be
That ere our hearts shall make

  Iago. Oh you are well tun'd now: But Ile set downe
the peggs that make this Musicke, as honest as I am

  Othe. Come: let vs to the Castle.
Newes (Friends) our Warres are done:
The Turkes are drown'd.
How do's my old Acquaintance of this Isle?
(Hony) you shall be well desir'd in Cyprus,
I haue found great loue among'st them. Oh my Sweet,
I prattle out of fashion, and I doate
In mine owne comforts. I prythee, good Iago,
Go to the Bay, and disimbarke my Coffers:
Bring thou the Master to the Cittadell,
He is a good one, and his worthynesse
Do's challenge much respect. Come Desdemona,
Once more well met at Cyprus.

Exit Othello and Desdemona.

Iago. Do thou meet me presently at the Harbour. Come thither, if thou be'st Valiant, (as they say base men being in Loue, haue then a Nobilitie in their Natures, more then is natiue to them) list-me; the Lieutenant to night watches on the Court of Guard. First, I must tell thee this: Desdemona, is directly in loue with him

Rod. With him? Why, 'tis not possible

Iago. Lay thy finger thus: and let thy soule be instructed. Marke me with what violence she first lou'd the Moore, but for bragging, and telling her fantasticall lies. To loue him still for prating, let not thy discreet heart thinke it. Her eye must be fed. And what delight shall she haue to looke on the diuell? When the Blood is made dull with the Act of Sport, there should be a game to enflame it, and to giue Satiety a fresh appetite. Louelinesse in fauour, simpathy in yeares, Manners, and Beauties: all which the Moore is defectiue in. Now for want of these requir'd Conueniences, her delicate tendernesse wil finde it selfe abus'd, begin to heaue the, gorge, disrellish and abhorre the Moore, very Nature wil instruct her in it, and compell her to some second choice. Now Sir, this granted (as it is a most pregnant and vnforc'd position) who stands so eminent in the degree of this Fortune, as Cassio do's: a knaue very voluble: no further conscionable, then in putting on the meere forme of Ciuill, and Humaine seeming, for the better compasse of his salt, and most hidden loose Affection? Why none, why none: A slipper, and subtle knaue, a finder of occasion: that he's an eye can stampe, and counterfeit Aduantages, though true Aduantage neuer present it selfe. A diuelish knaue: besides, the knaue is handsome, young: and hath all those requisites in him, that folly and greene mindes looke after. A pestilent compleat knaue, and the woman hath found him already

  Rodo. I cannot beleeue that in her, she's full of most bless'd
  condition

Iago. Bless'd figges-end. The Wine she drinkes is made of grapes. If shee had beene bless'd, shee would neuer haue lou'd the Moore: Bless'd pudding. Didst thou not see her paddle with the palme of his hand? Didst not marke that? Rod. Yes, that I did: but that was but curtesie

Iago . Leacherie by this hand: an Index, and obscure prologue to the
History of Lust and foule Thoughts. They met so neere with their lippes,
that their breathes embrac'd together. Villanous thoughts Rodorigo, when
these mutabilities so marshall the way, hard at hand comes the Master,
and maine exercise, th' incorporate conclusion: Pish. But Sir, be you rul'd
by me. I haue brought you from Venice. Watch you to night: for the
Command, Ile lay't vpon you. Cassio knowes you not: Ile not be farre from
you. Do you finde some occasion to anger Cassio, either by speaking too
loud, or tainting his discipline, or from what other course you please,
which the time shall more fauorably minister

Rod. Well

Iago. Sir, he's rash, and very sodaine in Choller: and happely may strike at
you, prouoke him that he may: for euen out of that will I cause these of
Cyprus to Mutiny. Whose qualification shall come into no true taste
againe, but by the displanting of Cassio. So shall you haue a shorter
iourney to your desires, by the meanes I shall then haue to preferre them.
And the impediment most profitably remoued, without the which there
were no expectation of our prosperitie

Rodo. I will do this, if you can bring it to any opportunity

   Iago. I warrant thee. Meete me by and by at the
Cittadell. I must fetch his Necessaries a Shore. Farewell

   Rodo. Adieu.
Enter.

   Iago. That Cassio loues her, I do well beleeu't:
That she loues him, 'tis apt, and of great Credite.
The Moore (howbeit that I endure him not)
Is of a constant, louing, Noble Nature,
And I dare thinke, he'le proue to Desdemona
A most deere husband. Now I do loue her too,
Not out of absolute Lust, (though peraduenture
I stand accomptant for as great a sin)
But partely led to dyet my Reuenge,
For that I do suspect the lustie Moore
Hath leap'd into my Seate. The thought whereof,
Doth (like a poysonous Minerall) gnaw my Inwardes:

And nothing can, or shall content my Soule
Till I am eeuen'd with him, wife, for wife.
Or fayling so, yet that I put the Moore,
At least into a Ielouzie so strong
That iudgement cannot cure. Which thing to do,
If this poore Trash of Venice, whom I trace
For his quicke hunting, stand the putting on,
Ile haue our Michael Cassio on the hip,
Abuse him to the Moore, in the right garbe
(For I feare Cassio with my Night-Cape too)
Make the Moore thanke me, loue me, and reward me,
For making him egregiously an Asse,
And practising vpon his peace, and quiet,
Euen to madnesse. 'Tis heere: but yet confus'd,
Knaueries plaine face, is neuer seene, till vs'd.
Enter.

Scena Secunda.

Enter Othello's Herald with a Proclamation.

Herald. It is Othello's pleasure, our Noble and Valiant Generall. That vpon
certaine tydings now arriu'd, importing the meere perdition of the
Turkish Fleete: euery man put himselfe into Triumph. Some to daunce,
some to make Bonfires, each man, to what Sport and Reuels his addition
leads him. For besides these beneficiall Newes, it is the Celebration of his
Nuptiall. So much was his pleasure should be proclaimed. All offices are
open, & there is full libertie of Feasting from this present houre of fiue, till
the Bell haue told eleuen. Blesse the Isle of Cyprus, and our Noble
Generall Othello. Enter.

Enter Othello, Desdemona, Cassio, and Attendants.

  Othe. Good Michael, looke you to the guard to night.
Let's teach our selues that Honourable stop,
Not to out-sport discretion

  Cas. Iago, hath direction what to do.
But notwithstanding with my personall eye
Will I looke to't

Othe. Iago, is most honest:
Michael, goodnight. To morrow with your earliest,
Let me haue speech with you. Come my deere Loue,
The purchase made, the fruites are to ensue,
That profit's yet to come 'tweene me, and you.
Goodnight.
Enter.

Enter Iago.

Cas. Welcome Iago: we must to the Watch

Iago. Not this houre Lieutenant: 'tis not yet ten o'th' clocke. Our Generall cast vs thus earely for the loue of his Desdemona: Who, let vs not therefore blame; he hath not yet made wanton the night with her: and she is sport for Ioue

Cas. She's a most exquisite Lady

Iago. And Ile warrant her, full of Game

Cas. Indeed shes a most fresh and delicate creature

Iago. What an eye she ha's?
Me thinkes it sounds a parley to prouocation

Cas. An inuiting eye:
And yet me thinkes right modest

Iago. And when she speakes,
Is it not an Alarum to Loue?
Cas. She is indeed perfection

Iago. Well: happinesse to their Sheetes. Come Lieutenant, I haue a stope of Wine, and heere without are a brace of Cyprus Gallants, that would faine haue a measure to the health of blacke Othello

Cas. Not to night, good Iago, I haue very poore, and vnhappie Braines for drinking. I could well wish Curtesie would inuent some other Custome of entertainment

Iago. Oh, they are our Friends: but one Cup, Ile drinke for you

Cassio. I haue drunke but one Cup to night, and that was craftily qualified too: and behold what inouation it makes heere. I am infortunate in the infirmity, and dare not taske my weakenesse with any more

   Iago. What man? 'Tis a night of Reuels, the Gallants desire it

   Cas. Where are they?
   Iago. Heere, at the doore: I pray you call them in

   Cas. Ile do't, but it dislikes me.
Enter.

   Iago. If I can fasten but one Cup vpon him
With that which he hath drunke to night alreadie,
He'l be as full of Quarrell, and offence
As my yong Mistris dogge.
Now my sicke Foole Rodorigo,
Whom Loue hath turn'd almost the wrong side out,
To Desdemona hath to night Carrows'd.
Potations, pottle-deepe; and he's to watch.
Three else of Cyprus, Noble swelling Spirites,
(That hold their Honours in a wary distance,
The very Elements of this Warrelike Isle)
Haue I to night fluster'd with flowing Cups,
And they Watch too.
Now 'mongst this Flocke of drunkards
Am I put to our Cassio in some Action
That may offend the Isle. But here they come.
Enter Cassio, Montano, and Gentlemen.

If Consequence do but approue my dreame,
My Boate sailes freely, both with winde and Streame

Cas. 'Fore heauen, they haue giuen me a rowse already

   Mon. Good-faith a litle one: not past a pint, as I am a Souldier

   Iago. Some Wine hoa.
And let me the Cannakin clinke, clinke:
And let me the Cannakin clinke.

A Souldiers a man: Oh, mans life's but a span,
Why then let a Souldier drinke.
Some Wine Boyes

Cas. 'Fore Heauen: an excellent Song

Iago. I learn'd it in England: where indeed they are most potent in Potting.
Your Dane, your Germaine, and your swag-belly'd Hollander, (drinke hoa)
are nothing to your English

  Cassio. Is your Englishmen so exquisite in his drinking?
  Iago. Why, he drinkes you with facillitie, your Dane
dead drunke. He sweates not to ouerthrow your Almaine.
He giues your Hollander a vomit, ere the next
Pottle can be fill'd

Cas. To the health of our Generall

Mon. I am for it Lieutenant: and Ile do you Iustice

  Iago. Oh sweet England.
King Stephen was anda worthy Peere,
His Breeches cost him but a Crowne,
He held them Six pence all to deere,
With that he cal'd the Tailor Lowne:
He was a wight of high Renowne,
And thou art but of low degree:
'Tis Pride that pulls the Country downe,
And take thy awl'd Cloake about thee.
Some Wine hoa

Cassio. Why this is a more exquisite Song then the other

Iago. Will you heare't againe? Cas. No: for I hold him to be vnworthy of
his Place, that do's those things. Well: heau'ns aboue all: and there be
soules must be saued, and there be soules must not be saued

Iago. It's true, good Lieutenant

  Cas. For mine owne part, no offence to the Generall, nor any man
  of qualitie: I hope to be saued

Iago. And so do I too Lieutenant

Cassio. I: (but by your leaue) not before me. The Lieutenant is to be saued
before the Ancient. Let's haue no more of this: let's to our Affaires.
Forgiue vs our sinnes: Gentlemen let's looke to our businesse. Do not
thinke Gentlemen, I am drunke: this is my Ancient, this is my right hand,
and this is my left. I am not drunke now: I can stand well enough, and I
speake well enough

Gent. Excellent well

   Cas. Why very well then: you must not thinke then,
that I am drunke.
Enter.

   Monta. To th' Platforme (Masters) come, let's set the
Watch

   Iago. You see this Fellow, that is gone before,
He's a Souldier, fit to stand by Caesar,
And giue direction. And do but see his vice,
'Tis to his vertue, a iust Equinox,
The one as long as th' other. 'Tis pittie of him:
I feare the trust Othello puts him in,
On some odde time of his infirmitie
Will shake this Island

   Mont. But is he often thus?
   Iago. 'Tis euermore his prologue to his sleepe,
He'le watch the Horologe a double Set,
If Drinke rocke not his Cradle

   Mont. It were well
The Generall were put in mind of it:
Perhaps he sees it not, or his good nature
Prizes the vertue that appeares in Cassio,
And lookes not on his euills: is not this true?
Enter Rodorigo.

   Iago. How now Rodorigo?
I pray you after the Lieutenant, go

Mon. And 'tis great pitty, that the Noble Moore
Should hazard such a Place, as his owne Second
With one of an ingraft Infirmitie,
It were an honest Action, to say so
To the Moore

Iago. Not I, for this faire Island,
I do loue Cassio well: and would do much
To cure him of this euill, But hearke, what noise?
Enter Cassio pursuing Rodorigo.

Cas. You Rogue: you Rascall

Mon. What's the matter Lieutenant?
Cas. A Knaue teach me my dutie? Ile beate the
Knaue in to a Twiggen-Bottle

Rod. Beate me?
Cas. Dost thou prate, Rogue?
Mon. Nay, good Lieutenant:
I pray you Sir, hold your hand

Cassio. Let me go (Sir)
Or Ile knocke you o're the Mazard

Mon. Come, come: you're drunke

Cassio. Drunke?
Iago. Away I say: go out and cry a Mutinie.
Nay good Lieutenant. Alas Gentlemen:
Helpe hoa. Lieutenant. Sir Montano:
Helpe Masters. Heere's a goodly Watch indeed.
Who's that which rings the Bell: Diablo, hoa:
The Towne will rise. Fie, fie Lieutenant,
You'le be asham'd for euer.
Enter Othello, and Attendants.

Othe. What is the matter heere?
Mon. I bleed still, I am hurt to th' death. He dies

Othe. Hold for your liues

Iag. Hold hoa: Lieutenant, Sir Montano, Gentlemen:
Haue you forgot all place of sense and dutie?
Hold. The Generall speaks to you: hold for shame

Oth. Why how now hoa? From whence ariseth this?
Are we turn'd Turkes? and to our selues do that
Which Heauen hath forbid the Ottamittes.
For Christian shame, put by this barbarous Brawle:
He that stirs next, to carue for his owne rage,
Holds his soule light: He dies vpon his Motion.
Silence that dreadfull Bell, it frights the Isle,
From her propriety. What is the matter, Masters?
Honest Iago, that lookes dead with greeuing,
Speake: who began this? On thy loue I charge thee?
    Iago. I do not know: Friends all, but now, euen now.
In Quarter, and in termes like Bride, and Groome
Deuesting them for Bed: and then, but now:
(As if some Planet had vnwitted men)
Swords out, and tilting one at others breastes,
In opposition bloody. I cannot speake
Any begining to this peeuish oddes.
And would, in Action glorious, I had lost
Those legges, that brought me to a part of it

    Othe. How comes it (Michaell) you are thus forgot?
    Cas. I pray you pardon me, I cannot speake

    Othe. Worthy Montano, you were wont to be ciuill:
The grauitie, and stillnesse of your youth
The world hath noted. And your name is great
In mouthes of wisest Censure. What's the matter
That you vnlace your reputation thus,
And spend your rich opinion, for the name
Of a night-brawler? Giue me answer to it

    Mon. Worthy Othello, I am hurt to danger,
Your Officer Iago, can informe you,
While I spare speech which something now offends me.
Of all that I do know, nor know I ought
By me, that's said, or done amisse this night,
Vnlesse selfe-charitie be sometimes a vice,

And to defend our selues, it be a sinne
When violence assailes vs

  Othe. Now by Heauen,
My blood begins my safer Guides to rule,
And passion (hauing my best iudgement collied)
Assaies to leade the way. If I once stir,
Or do but lift this Arme, the best of you
Shall sinke in my rebuke. Giue me to know
How this foule Rout began: Who set it on,
And he that is approu'd in this offence,
Though he had twinn'd with me, both at a birth,
Shall loose me. What in a Towne of warre,
Yet wilde, the peoples hearts brim-full of feare,
To Manage priuate, and domesticke Quarrell?
In night, and on the Court and Guard of safetie?
'Tis monstrous: Iago, who began't?
  Mon. If partially Affin'd, or league in office,
Thou dost deliuer more, or lesse then Truth,
Thou art no Souldier

  Iago. Touch me not so neere,
I had rather haue this tongue cut from my mouth,
Then it should do offence to Michaell Cassio.
Yet I perswade my selfe, to speake the truth
Shall nothing wrong him. This it is Generall:
Montano and my selfe being in speech,
There comes a Fellow, crying out for helpe,
And Cassio following him with determin'd Sword
To execute vpon him. Sir, this Gentleman,
Steppes in to Cassio, and entreats his pause:
My selfe, the crying Fellow did pursue,
Least by his clamour (as it so fell out)
The Towne might fall in fright. He, (swift of foote)
Out-ran my purpose: and I return'd then rather
For that I heard the clinke, and fall of Swords,
And Cassio high in oath: Which till to night
I nere might say before. When I came backe
(For this was briefe) I found them close together
At blow, and thrust, euen as againe they were
When you your selfe did part them.

More of this matter cannot I report,
But Men are Men: The best sometimes forget,
Though Cassio did some little wrong to him,
As men in rage strike those that wish them best,
Yet surely Cassio, I beleeue receiu'd
From him that fled, some strange Indignitie,
Which patience could not passe

  Othe. I know Iago
Thy honestie, and loue doth mince this matter,
Making it light to Cassio: Cassio, I loue thee,
But neuer more be Officer of mine.
Enter Desdemona attended.

Looke if my gentle Loue be not rais'd vp:
Ile make thee an example

  Des. What is the matter (Deere?)
  Othe. All's well, Sweeting:
Come away to bed. Sir for your hurts,
My selfe will be your Surgeon. Lead him off:
Iago, looke with care about the Towne,
And silence those whom this vil'd brawle distracted.
Come Desdemona, 'tis the Soldiers life,
To haue their Balmy slumbers wak'd with strife.
Enter.

  Iago. What are you hurt Lieutenant?
  Cas. I, past all Surgery

Iago. Marry Heauen forbid

Cas. Reputation, Reputation, Reputation: Oh I haue lost my Reputation. I haue lost the immortall part of myselfe, and what remaines is bestiall. My Reputation, Iago, my Reputation

Iago. As I am an honest man I had thought you had receiued some bodily wound; there is more sence in that then in Reputation. Reputation is an idle, and most false imposition; oft got without merit, and lost without deseruing. You haue lost no Reputation at all, vnlesse you repute your selfe such a looser. What man, there are more wayes to recouer the Generall againe. You are but now cast in his moode, (a punishment more

in policie, then in malice) euen so as one would beate his offencelesse
dogge, to affright an Imperious Lyon. Sue to him againe, and he's yours

Cas. I will rather sue to be despis'd, then to deceiue so good a
Commander, with so slight, so drunken, and so indiscreet an Officer.
Drunke? And speake Parrat? And squabble? Swagger? Sweare? And
discourse Fustian with ones owne shadow? Oh thou invisible spirit of
Wine, if thou hast no name to be knowne by, let vs call thee Diuell

   Iago. What was he that you follow'd with your
Sword? What had he done to you?
   Cas. I know not

Iago. Is't possible? Cas. I remember a masse of things, but nothing
distinctly: a Quarrell, but nothing wherefore. Oh, that men should put an
Enemie in their mouthes, to steale away their Braines? that we should
with ioy, pleasance, reuell and applause, transforme our selues into Beasts

Iago. Why? But you are now well enough: how came you thus recouered?
Cas. It hath pleas'd the diuell drunkennesse, to giue place to the diuell
wrath, one vnperfectnesse, shewes me another to make me frankly
despise my selfe

   Iago. Come, you are too seuere a Moraller. As the
Time, the Place, & the Condition of this Country stands
I could hartily wish this had not befalne: but since it is, as
it is, mend it for your owne good

Cas. I will aske him for my Place againe, he shall tell me, I am a drunkard:
had I as many mouthes as Hydra, such an answer would stop them all. To
be now a sensible man, by and by a Foole, and presently a Beast. Oh
strange! Euery inordinate cup is vnbless'd, and the Ingredient is a diuell

   Iago. Come, come: good wine, is a good familiar
Creature, if it be well vs'd: exclaime no more against it.
And good Lieutenant, I thinke, you thinke I loue
you

Cassio. I haue well approued it, Sir. I drunke? Iago. You, or any man
liuing, may be drunke at a time man. I tell you what you shall do: Our
General's Wife, is now the Generall. I may say so, in this respect, for that
he hath deuoted, and giuen vp himselfe to the Contemplation, marke: and

deuotement of her parts and Graces. Confesse your selfe freely to her: Importune her helpe to put you in your place againe. She is of so free, so kinde, so apt, so blessed a disposition, she holds it a vice in her goodnesse, not to do more then she is requested. This broken ioynt betweene you, and her husband, entreat her to splinter. And my Fortunes against any lay worth naming, this cracke of your Loue, shall grow stronger, then it was before

Cassio. You aduise me well

    Iago. I protest in the sinceritie of Loue, and honest kindnesse

Cassio. I thinke it freely: and betimes in the morning, I will beseech the vertuous Desdemona to vndertake for me: I am desperate of my Fortunes if they check me

    Iago. You are in the right: good night Lieutenant, I must to the Watch

Cassio. Good night, honest Iago.

Exit Cassio.

  Iago. And what's he then,
That saies I play the Villaine?
When this aduise is free I giue, and honest,
Proball to thinking, and indeed the course
To win the Moore againe.
For 'tis most easie
Th' inclyning Desdemona to subdue
In any honest Suite. She's fram'd as fruitefull
As the free Elements. And then for her
To win the Moore, were to renownce his Baptisme,
All Seales, and Simbols of redeemed sin:
His Soule is so enfetter'd to her Loue,
That she may make, vnmake, do what she list,
Euen as her Appetite shall play the God,
With his weake Function. How am I then a Villaine,
To Counsell Cassio to this paralell course,
Directly to his good? Diuinitie of hell,
When diuels will the blackest sinnes put on,
They do suggest at first with heauenly shewes,

As I do now. For whiles this honest Foole
Plies Desdemona, to repaire his Fortune,
And she for him, pleades strongly to the Moore,
Ile powre this pestilence into his eare:
That she repeales him, for her bodies Lust,
And by how much she striues to do him good,
She shall vndo her Credite with the Moore.
So will I turne her vertue into pitch.
And out of her owne goodnesse make the Net,
That shall en-mash them all.
How now Rodorigo?
Enter Rodorigo.

Rodorigo. I do follow heere in the Chace, not like a Hound that hunts, but
one that filles vp the Crie. My Money is almost spent; I haue bin to night
exceedingly well Cudgell'd: And I thinke the issue will bee, I shall haue so
much experience for my paines; And so, with no money at all, and a little
more Wit, returne againe to Venice

   Iago. How poore are they that haue not Patience?
What wound did euer heale but by degrees?
Thou know'st we worke by Wit, and not by Witchcraft
And Wit depends on dilatory time:
Dos't not go well? Cassio hath beaten thee,
And thou by that small hurt hath casheer'd Cassio:
Though other things grow faire against the Sun,
Yet Fruites that blossome first, will first be ripe:
Content thy selfe, a-while. Introth 'tis Morning;
Pleasure, and Action, make the houres seeme short.
Retire thee, go where thou art Billited:
Away, I say, thou shalt know more heereafter:
Nay get thee gone.

Exit Roderigo.

Two things are to be done:
My Wife must moue for Cassio to her Mistris:
Ile set her on my selfe, a while, to draw the Moor apart,
And bring him iumpe, when he may Cassio finde
Soliciting his wife: I, that's the way:

Dull not Deuice, by coldnesse, and delay.
Enter.

Actus Tertius. Scena Prima.

Enter Cassio, Musitians, and Clowne.

  Cassio. Masters, play heere, I wil content your paines,
Something that's briefe: and bid, goodmorrow General

  Clo. Why Masters, haue your Instruments bin in Naples,
that they speake i'th' Nose thus?
  Mus. How Sir? how?
  Clo. Are these I pray you, winde Instruments?
  Mus. I marry are they sir

Clo. Oh, thereby hangs a tale

Mus. Whereby hangs a tale, sir? Clow. Marry sir, by many a winde
Instrument that I know. But Masters, heere's money for you: and the
Generall so likes your Musick, that he desires you for loues sake to make
no more noise with it

Mus. Well Sir, we will not

Clo. If you haue any Musicke that may not be heard, too't againe. But (as
they say) to heare Musicke, the Generall do's not greatly care

Mus. We haue none such, sir

  Clow. Then put vp your Pipes in your bagge, for Ile away. Go,
  vanish into ayre, away.

Exit Mu.

  Cassio. Dost thou heare me, mine honest Friend?
  Clo. No, I heare not your honest Friend:
I heare you

Cassio. Prythee keepe vp thy Quillets, ther's a poore peece of Gold for
thee: if the Gentlewoman that attends the Generall be stirring, tell her,
there's one Cassio entreats her a little fauour of Speech. Wilt thou do this?

Clo. She is stirring sir: if she will stirre hither, I shall seeme to notifie vnto her.

Exit Clo.

Enter Iago.

In happy time, Iago

  Iago. You haue not bin a-bed then?
  Cassio. Why no: the day had broke before we parted.
I haue made bold (Iago) to send in to your wife:
My suite to her is, that she will to vertuous Desdemona
Procure me some accesse

  Iago. Ile send her to you presently:
And Ile deuise a meane to draw the Moore
Out of the way, that your conuerse and businesse
May be more free.

Exit

  Cassio. I humbly thanke you for't. I neuer knew
A Florentine more kinde, and honest.
Enter aemilia.

Aemil. Goodmorrow (good Lieutenant) I am sorrie
For your displeasure: but all will sure be well.
The Generall and his wife are talking of it,
And she speakes for you stoutly. The Moore replies,
That he you hurt is of great Fame in Cyprus,
And great Affinitie: and that in wholsome Wisedome
He might not but refuse you. But he protests he loues you
And needs no other Suitor, but his likings
To bring you in againe

  Cassio. Yet I beseech you,
If you thinke fit, or that it may be done,
Giue me aduantage of some breefe Discourse
With Desdemon alone.
Aemil. Pray you come in:

I will bestow you where you shall haue time
To speake your bosome freely

Cassio. I am much bound to you.

Scoena Secunda.

Enter Othello, Iago, and Gentlemen.

  Othe. These Letters giue (Iago) to the Pylot,
And by him do my duties to the Senate:
That done, I will be walking on the Workes,
Repaire there to mee

Iago. Well, my good Lord, Ile doo't

  Oth. This Fortification (Gentlemen) shall we see't?
  Gent. Well waite vpon your Lordship.

Exeunt.

Scoena Tertia.

Enter Desdemona, Cassio, and aemilia.

  Des. Be thou assur'd (good Cassio) I will do
All my abilities in thy behalfe.
Aemil. Good Madam do:
I warrant it greeues my Husband,
As if the cause were his

  Des. Oh that's an honest Fellow, Do not doubt Cassio
But I will haue my Lord, and you againe
As friendly as you were

  Cassio. Bounteous Madam,
What euer shall become of Michael Cassio,
He's neuer any thing but your true Seruant

  Des. I know't: I thanke you: you do loue my Lord:
You haue knowne him long, and be you well assur'd
He shall in strangenesse stand no farther off,
Then in a politique distance

Cassio. I, but Lady,
That policie may either last so long,
Or feede vpon such nice and waterish diet,
Or breede it selfe so out of Circumstances,
That I being absent, and my place supply'd,
My Generall will forget my Loue, and Seruice

Des. Do not doubt that: before aemilia here,
I giue thee warrant of thy place. Assure thee,
If I do vow a friendship, Ile performe it
To the last Article. My Lord shall neuer rest,
Ile watch him tame, and talke him out of patience;
His Bed shall seeme a Schoole, his Boord a Shrift,
Ile intermingle euery thing he do's
With Cassio's suite: Therefore be merry Cassio,
For thy Solicitor shall rather dye,
Then giue thy cause away.
Enter Othello, and Iago.

Aemil. Madam, heere comes my Lord

Cassio. Madam, Ile take my leaue

Des. Why stay, and heare me speake

Cassio. Madam, not now: I am very ill at ease,
Vnfit for mine owne purposes

Des. Well, do your discretion.

Exit Cassio.

Iago. Hah? I like not that

Othel. What dost thou say?
Iago. Nothing my Lord; or if- I know not what

Othel. Was not that Cassio parted from my wife?
Iago. Cassio my Lord? No sure, I cannot thinke it
That he would steale away so guilty-like,
Seeing your comming

Oth. I do beleeue 'twas he

  Des. How now my Lord?
I haue bin talking with a Suitor heere,
A man that languishes in your displeasure

  Oth. Who is't you meane?
  Des. Why your Lieutenant Cassio: Good my Lord,
If I haue any grace, or power to moue you,
His present reconciliation take.
For if he be not one, that truly loues you,
That erres in Ignorance, and not in Cunning,
I haue no iudgement in an honest face.
I prythee call him backe

  Oth. Went he hence now?
  Des. I sooth; so humbled,
That he hath left part of his greefe with mee
To suffer with him. Good Loue, call him backe

Othel. Not now (sweet Desdemon) some other time

  Des. But shall't be shortly?
  Oth. The sooner (Sweet) for you

  Des. Shall't be to night, at Supper?
  Oth. No, not to night

  Des. To morrow Dinner then?
  Oth. I shall not dine at home:
I meete the Captaines at the Cittadell

  Des. Why then to morrow night, on Tuesday morne,
On Tuesday noone, or night; on Wensday Morne.
I prythee name the time, but let it not
Exceed three dayes. Infaith hee's penitent:
And yet his Trespasse, in our common reason
(Saue that they say the warres must make example)
Out of her best, is not almost a fault
T' encurre a priuate checke. When shall he come?
Tell me Othello. I wonder in my Soule
What you would aske me, that I should deny,

Or stand so mam'ring on? What? Michael Cassio,
That came a woing with you? and so many a time
(When I haue spoke of you dispraisingly)
Hath tane your part, to haue so much to do
To bring him in? Trust me, I could do much

   Oth. Prythee no more: Let him come when he will:
I will deny thee nothing

   Des. Why, this is not a Boone:
'Tis as I should entreate you weare your Gloues,
Or feede on nourishing dishes, or keepe you warme,
Or sue to you, to do a peculiar profit
To your owne person. Nay, when I haue a suite
Wherein I meane to touch your Loue indeed,
It shall be full of poize, and difficult waight,
And fearefull to be granted

   Oth. I will deny thee nothing.
Whereon, I do beseech thee, grant me this,
To leaue me but a little to my selfe

Des. Shall I deny you? No: farewell my Lord

Oth. Farewell my Desdemona, Ile come to thee strait

   Des. aemilia come; be as your Fancies teach you:
What ere you be, I am obedient.
Enter.

   Oth. Excellent wretch: Perdition catch my Soule
But I do loue thee: and when I loue thee not,
Chaos is come againe

Iago. My Noble Lord

   Oth. What dost thou say, Iago?
   Iago. Did Michael Cassio
When he woo'd my Lady, know of your loue?
   Oth. He did, from first to last:
Why dost thou aske?

Iago. But for a satisfaction of my Thought,
No further harme

   Oth. Why of thy thought, Iago?
Iago. I did not thinke he had bin acquainted with hir

Oth. O yes, and went betweene vs very oft

   Iago. Indeed?
   Oth. Indeed? I indeed. Discern'st thou ought in that?
Is he not honest?
   Iago. Honest, my Lord?
   Oth. Honest? I, Honest

Iago. My Lord, for ought I know

   Oth. What do'st thou thinke?
   Iago. Thinke, my Lord?
   Oth. Thinke, my Lord? Alas, thou ecchos't me;
As if there were some Monster in thy thought
Too hideous to be shewne. Thou dost mean somthing:
I heard thee say euen now, thou lik'st not that,
When Cassio left my wife. What didd'st not like?
And when I told thee, he was of my Counsaile,
Of my whole course of wooing; thou cried'st, Indeede?
And didd'st contract, and purse thy brow together,
As if thou then hadd'st shut vp in thy Braine
Some horrible Conceite. If thou do'st loue me,
Shew me thy thought

Iago. My Lord, you know I loue you

   Oth. I thinke thou do'st:
And for I know thou'rt full of Loue, and Honestie,
And weigh'st thy words before thou giu'st them breath,
Therefore these stops of thine, fright me the more:
For such things in a false disloyall Knaue
Are trickes of Custome: but in a man that's iust,
They're close dilations, working from the heart,
That Passion cannot rule

Iago. For Michael Cassio,
I dare be sworne, I thinke that he is honest

Oth. I thinke so too

Iago. Men should be what they seeme,
Or those that be not, would they might seeme none

Oth. Certaine, men should be what they seeme

Iago. Why then I thinke Cassio's an honest man

Oth. Nay, yet there's more in this?
I prythee speake to me, as to thy thinkings,
As thou dost ruminate, and giue thy worst of thoughts
The worst of words

Iago. Good my Lord pardon me,
Though I am bound to euery Acte of dutie,
I am not bound to that: All Slaues are free:
Vtter my Thoughts? Why say, they are vild, and falce?
As where's that Palace, whereinto foule things
Sometimes intrude not? Who ha's that breast so pure,
Wherein vncleanly Apprehensions
Keepe Leetes, and Law-dayes, and in Sessions sit
With meditations lawfull?
Oth. Thou do'st conspire against thy Friend (Iago)
If thou but think'st him wrong'd, and mak'st his eare
A stranger to thy Thoughts

Iago. I do beseech you,
Though I perchance am vicious in my guesse
(As I confesse it is my Natures plague
To spy into Abuses, and of my iealousie
Shapes faults that are not) that your wisedome
From one, that so imperfectly conceits,
Would take no notice, nor build your selfe a trouble
Out of his scattering, and vnsure obseruance:
It were not for your quiet, nor your good,
Nor for my Manhood, Honesty, and Wisedome,
To let you know my thoughts

Oth. What dost thou meane?

Iago. Good name in Man, & woman (deere my Lord)
Is the immediate Iewell of their Soules;
Who steales my purse, steales trash:
'Tis something, nothing;
'Twas mine, 'tis his, and has bin slaue to thousands:
But he that filches from me my good Name,
Robs me of that, which not enriches him,
And makes me poore indeed

Oth. Ile know thy Thoughts

Iago. You cannot, if my heart were in your hand,
Nor shall not, whil'st 'tis in my custodie

Oth. Ha?

Iago. Oh, beware my Lord, of iealousie,
It is the greene-ey'd Monster, which doth mocke
The meate it feeds on. That Cuckold liues in blisse,
Who certaine of his Fate, loues not his wronger:
But oh, what damned minutes tels he ore,
Who dotes, yet doubts: Suspects, yet soundly loues?

Oth. O miserie

Iago. Poore, and Content, is rich, and rich enough,
But Riches finelesse, is as poore as Winter,
To him that euer feares he shall be poore:
Good Heauen, the Soules of all my Tribe defend
From Iealousie

Oth. Why? why is this?
Think'st thou, I'ld make a Life of Iealousie;
To follow still the changes of the Moone
With fresh suspitions? No: to be once in doubt,
Is to be resolu'd: Exchange me for a Goat,
When I shall turne the businesse of my Soule
To such exufflicate, and blow'd Surmises,
Matching thy inference. 'Tis not to make me Iealious,
To say my wife is faire, feeds well, loues company,
Is free of Speech, Sings, Playes, and Dances:
Where Vertue is, these are more vertuous.

Nor from mine owne weake merites, will I draw
The smallest feare, or doubt of her reuolt,
For she had eyes, and chose me. No Iago,
Ile see before I doubt; when I doubt, proue;
And on the proofe, there is no more but this,
Away at once with Loue, or Iealousie

    Ia. I am glad of this: For now I shall haue reason
To shew the Loue and Duty that I beare you
With franker spirit. Therefore (as I am bound)
Receiue it from me. I speake not yet of proofe:
Looke to your wife, obserue her well with Cassio,
Weare your eyes, thus: not Iealious, nor Secure:
I would not haue your free, and Noble Nature,
Out of selfe-Bounty, be abus'd: Looke too't:
I know our Country disposition well:
In Venice, they do let Heauen see the prankes
They dare not shew their Husbands.
Their best Conscience,
Is not to leaue't vndone, but kept vnknowne

    Oth. Dost thou say so?
    Iago. She did deceiue her Father, marrying you,
And when she seem'd to shake, and feare your lookes,
She lou'd them most

Oth. And so she did

    Iago. Why go too then:
Shee that so young could giue out such a Seeming
To seele her Fathers eyes vp, close as Oake,
He thought 'twas Witchcraft.
But I am much too blame:
I humbly do beseech you of your pardon
For too much louing you

Oth. I am bound to thee for euer

    Iago. I see this hath a little dash'd your Spirits:
    Oth. Not a iot, not a iot

Iago. Trust me, I feare it has:
I hope you will consider what is spoke
Comes from your Loue.
But I do see y'are moou'd:
I am to pray you, not to straine my speech
To grosser issues, nor to larger reach,
Then to Suspition

Oth. I will not

Iago. Should you do so (my Lord)
My speech should fall into such vilde successe,
Which my Thoughts aym'd not.
Cassio's my worthy Friend:
My Lord, I see y'are mou'd

Oth. No, not much mou'd:
I do not thinke but Desdemona's honest

Iago. Long liue she so;
And long liue you to thinke so

Oth. And yet how Nature erring from it selfe

Iago. I, there's the point:
As (to be bold with you)
Not to affect many proposed Matches
Of her owne Clime, Complexion, and Degree,
Whereto we see in all things, Nature tends:
Foh, one may smel in such, a will most ranke,
Foule disproportions, Thoughts vnnaturall.
But (pardon me) I do not in position
Distinctly speake of her, though I may feare
Her will, recoyling to her better iudgement,
May fal to match you with her Country formes,
And happily repent

Oth. Farewell, farewell:
If more thou dost perceiue, let me know more:
Set on thy wife to obserue.
Leaue me Iago

Iago. My Lord, I take my leaue

  Othel. Why did I marry?
This honest Creature (doubtlesse)
Sees, and knowes more, much more then he vnfolds

  Iago. My Lord, I would I might intreat your Honor
To scan this thing no farther: Leaue it to time,
Although 'tis fit that Cassio haue his Place;
For sure he filles it vp with great Ability;
Yet if you please, to him off a-while:
You shall by that perceiue him, and his meanes:
Note if your Lady straine his Entertainment
With any strong, or vehement importunitie,
Much will be seene in that: In the meane time,
Let me be thought too busie in my feares,
(As worthy cause I haue to feare I am)
And hold her free, I do beseech your Honor

Oth. Feare not my gouernment

  Iago. I once more take my leaue.
Enter.

  Oth. This Fellow's of exceeding honesty,
And knowes all Quantities with a learn'd Spirit
Of humane dealings. If I do proue her Haggard,
Though that her Iesses were my deere heart-strings,
I'ld whistle her off, and let her downe the winde
To prey at Fortune. Haply, for I am blacke,
And haue not those soft parts of Conuersation
That Chamberers haue: Or for I am declin'd
Into the vale of yeares (yet that's not much)
Shee's gone. I am abus'd, and my releefe
Must be to loath her. Oh Curse of Marriage!
That we can call these delicate Creatures ours,
And not their Appetites? I had rather be a Toad,
And liue vpon the vapour of a Dungeon,
Then keepe a corner in the thing I loue
For others vses. Yet 'tis the plague to Great-ones,
Prerogatiu'd are they lesse then the Base,

'Tis destiny vnshunnable, like death:
Euen then, this forked plague is Fated to vs,
When we do quicken. Looke where she comes:
Enter Desdemona and aemilia.

If she be false, Heauen mock'd it selfe:
Ile not beleeue't

   Des. How now, my deere Othello?
Your dinner, and the generous Islanders
By you inuited, do attend your presence

Oth. I am too blame

   Des. Why do you speake so faintly?
Are you not well?
  Oth. I haue a paine vpon my Forehead, heere

   Des. Why that's with watching, 'twill away againe.
Let me but binde it hard, within this houre
It will be well

   Oth. Your Napkin is too little:
Let it alone: Come, Ile go in with you.
Enter.

   Des. I am very sorry that you are not well.
Aemil. I am glad I haue found this Napkin:
This was her first remembrance from the Moore,
My wayward Husband hath a hundred times
Woo'd me to steale it. But she so loues the Token,
(For he coniur'd her, she should euer keepe it)
That she reserues it euermore about her,
To kisse, and talke too. Ile haue the worke tane out,
And giu't Iago: what he will do with it
Heauen knowes, not I:
I nothing, but to please his Fantasie.
Enter Iago.

  Iago. How now? What do you heere alone?
Aemil. Do not you chide: I haue a thing for you

Iago. You haue a thing for me?
It is a common thing-
Aemil. Hah?
  Iago. To haue a foolish wife.
Aemil. Oh, is that all? What will you giue me now
For that same Handkerchiefe

  Iago. What Handkerchiefe?
Aemil. What Handkerchiefe?
Why that the Moore first gaue to Desdemona,
That which so often you did bid me steale

  Iago. Hast stolne it from her?
Aemil. No: but she let it drop by negligence,
And to th' aduantage, I being heere, took't vp:
Looke, heere 'tis

  Iago. A good wench, giue it me.
Aemil. What will you do with't, that you haue bene
so earnest to haue me filch it?
  Iago. Why, what is that to you?
Aemil. If it be not for some purpose of import,
Giu't me againe. Poore Lady, shee'l run mad
When she shall lacke it

  Iago. Be not acknowne on't:
I haue vse for it. Go, leaue me.

Exit aemil.

I will in Cassio's Lodging loose this Napkin,
And let him finde it. Trifles light as ayre,
Are to the iealious, confirmations strong,
As proofes of holy Writ. This may do something.
The Moore already changes with my poyson:
Dangerous conceites, are in their Natures poysons,
Which at the first are scarse found to distaste:
But with a little acte vpon the blood,
Burne like the Mines of Sulphure. I did say so.
Enter Othello.

Looke where he comes: Not Poppy, nor Mandragora,
Nor all the drowsie Syrrups of the world
Shall euer medicine thee to that sweete sleepe
Which thou owd'st yesterday

  Oth. Ha, ha, false to mee?
  Iago. Why how now Generall? No more of that

  Oth. Auant, be gone: Thou hast set me on the Racke:
I sweare 'tis better to be much abus'd,
Then but to know't a little

  Iago. How now, my Lord?
  Oth. What sense had I, in her stolne houres of Lust?
I saw't not, thought it not: it harm'd not me:
I slept the next night well, fed well, was free, and merrie.
I found not Cassio's kisses on her Lippes:
He that is robb'd, not wanting what is stolne,
Let him not know't, and he's not robb'd at all

  Iago. I am sorry to heare this?
  Oth. I had beene happy, if the generall Campe,
Pyoners and all, had tasted her sweet Body,
So I had nothing knowne. Oh now, for euer
Farewell the Tranquill minde; farewell Content;
Farewell the plumed Troopes, and the bigge Warres,
That makes Ambition, Vertue! Oh farewell,
Farewell the neighing Steed, and the shrill Trumpe,
The Spirit-stirring Drum, th' Eare-piercing Fife,
The Royall Banner, and all Qualitie,
Pride, Pompe, and Circumstance of glorious Warre:
And O you mortall Engines, whose rude throates
Th' immortall Ioues dread Clamours, counterfet,
Farewell: Othello's Occupation's gone

  Iago. Is't possible my Lord?
  Oth. Villaine, be sure thou proue my Loue a Whore;
Be sure of it: Giue me the Occular proofe,
Or by the worth of mine eternall Soule,
Thou had'st bin better haue bin borne a Dog
Then answer my wak'd wrath

Iago. Is't come to this?

  Oth. Make me to see't: or (at the least) so proue it,
That the probation beare no Hindge, nor Loope,
To hang a doubt on: Or woe vpon thy life

Iago. My Noble Lord

  Oth. If thou dost slander her, and torture me,
Neuer pray more: Abandon all remorse
On Horrors head, Horrors accumulate:
Do deeds to make Heauen weepe, all Earth amaz'd;
For nothing canst thou to damnation adde,
Greater then that

  Iago. O Grace! O Heauen forgiue me!
Are you a Man? Haue you a Soule? or Sense?
God buy you: take mine Office. Oh wretched Foole,
That lou'st to make thine Honesty, a Vice!
Oh monstrous world! Take note, take note (O World)
To be direct and honest, is not safe.
I thanke you for this profit, and from hence
Ile loue no Friend, sith Loue breeds such offence

Oth. Nay stay: thou should'st be honest

  Iago. I should be wise; for Honestie's a Foole,
And looses that it workes for

  Oth. By the World,
I thinke my Wife be honest, and thinke she is not:
I thinke that thou art iust, and thinke thou art not:
Ile haue some proofe. My name that was as fresh
As Dians Visage, is now begrim'd and blacke
As mine owne face. If there be Cords, or Kniues,
Poyson, or Fire, or suffocating streames,
Ile not indure it. Would I were satisfied

  Iago. I see you are eaten vp with Passion:
I do repent me, that I put it to you.
You would be satisfied?
  Oth. Would? Nay, and I will

Iago. And may: but how? How satisfied, my Lord?
Would you the super-vision grossely gape on?
Behold her top'd?
  Oth. Death, and damnation. Oh!
  Iago. It were a tedious difficulty, I thinke,
To bring them to that Prospect: Damne them then,
If euer mortall eyes do see them boulster
More then their owne. What then? How then?
What shall I say? Where's Satisfaction?
It is impossible you should see this,
Were they as prime as Goates, as hot as Monkeyes,
As salt as Wolues in pride, and Fooles as grosse
As Ignorance, made drunke. But yet, I say,
If imputation, and strong circumstances,
Which leade directly to the doore of Truth,
Will giue you satisfaction, you might haue't

Oth. Giue me a liuing reason she's disloyall

  Iago. I do not like the Office.
But sith I am entred in this cause so farre
(Prick'd too't by foolish Honesty, and Loue)
I will go on. I lay with Cassio lately,
And being troubled with a raging tooth,
I could not sleepe. There are a kinde of men,
So loose of Soule, that in their sleepes will mutter
Their Affayres: one of this kinde is Cassio:
In sleepe I heard him say, sweet Desdemona,
Let vs be wary, let vs hide our Loues,
And then (Sir) would he gripe, and wring my hand:
Cry, oh sweet Creature: then kisse me hard,
As if he pluckt vp kisses by the rootes,
That grew vpon my lippes, laid his Leg ore my Thigh,
And sigh, and kisse, and then cry cursed Fate,
That gaue thee to the Moore

  Oth. O monstrous! monstrous!
  Iago. Nay, this was but his Dreame

  Oth. But this denoted a fore-gone conclusion,
'Tis a shrew'd doubt, though it be but a Dreame

Iago. And this may helpe to thicken other proofes,
That do demonstrate thinly

Oth. Ile teare her all to peeces

Iago. Nay yet be wise; yet we see nothing done,
She may be honest yet: Tell me but this,
Haue you not sometimes seene a Handkerchiefe
Spotted with Strawberries, in your wiues hand?
  Oth. I gaue her such a one: 'twas my first gift

Iago. I know not that: but such a Handkerchiefe
(I am sure it was your wiues) did I to day
See Cassio wipe his Beard with

Oth. If it be that

Iago. If it be that, or any, it was here.
It speakes against her with the other proofes

  Othel. O that the Slaue had forty thousand liues:
One is too poore, too weake for my reuenge.
Now do I see 'tis true. Looke heere Iago,
All my fond loue thus do I blow to Heauen. 'Tis gone.
Arise blacke vengeance, from the hollow hell,
Yeeld vp (O Loue) thy Crowne, and hearted Throne
To tyrannous Hate. Swell bosome with thy fraught,
For 'tis of Aspickes tongues

Iago. Yet be content

Oth. Oh blood, blood, blood

Iago. Patience I say: your minde may change

  Oth. Neuer Iago. Like to the Ponticke Sea,
Whose Icie Current, and compulsiue course,
Neu'r keepes retyring ebbe, but keepes due on
To the Proponticke, and the Hellespont:
Euen so my bloody thoughts, with violent pace
Shall neu'r looke backe, neu'r ebbe to humble Loue,
Till that a capeable, and wide Reuenge

Swallow them vp. Now by yond Marble Heauen,
In the due reuerence of a Sacred vow,
I heere engage my words

  Iago. Do not rise yet:
Witnesse you euer-burning Lights aboue,
You Elements, that clip vs round about,
Witnesse that heere Iago doth giue vp
The execution of his wit, hands, heart,
To wrong'd Othello's Seruice. Let him command,
And to obey shall be in me remorse,
What bloody businesse euer

  Oth. I greet thy loue,
Not with vaine thanks, but with acceptance bounteous,
And will vpon the instant put thee too't.
Within these three dayes let me heare thee say,
That Cassio's not aliue

  Iago. My Friend is dead:
'Tis done at your Request.
But let her liue

  Oth. Damne her lewde Minx:
O damne her, damne her.
Come go with me a-part, I will withdraw
To furnish me with some swift meanes of death
For the faire Diuell.
Now art thou my Lieutenant

Iago. I am your owne for euer.

Exeunt.

Scaena Quarta.

Enter Desdemona, aemilia, and Clown.

  Des. Do you know Sirrah, where Lieutenant Cassio
lyes?
  Clow. I dare not say he lies any where

Des. Why man?

Clo. He's a Soldier, and for me to say a Souldier lyes,
'tis stabbing

Des. Go too: where lodges he?

Clo. To tell you where he lodges, is to tel you where
I lye

Des. Can any thing be made of this?

Clo. I know not where he lodges, and for mee to deuise
a lodging, and say he lies heere, or he lies there, were
to lye in mine owne throat

Des. Can you enquire him out? and be edified by report?

Clo. I will Catechize the world for him, that is, make
Questions, and by them answer

Des. Seeke him, bidde him come hither: tell him, I haue moou'd my Lord
on his behalfe, and hope all will be well

Clo. To do this, is within the compasse of mans Wit,
and therefore I will attempt the doing it.

Exit Clo.

Des. Where should I loose the Handkerchiefe, aemilia?

Aemil. I know not Madam

Des. Beleeue me, I had rather haue lost my purse
Full of Cruzadoes. And but my Noble Moore
Is true of minde, and made of no such basenesse,
As iealious Creatures are, it were enough
To put him to ill-thinking.

Aemil. Is he not iealious?

Des. Who, he? I thinke the Sun where he was borne,
Drew all such humors from him.

Aemil. Looke where he comes.

Enter Othello.

Des. I will not leaue him now, till Cassio be
Call'd to him. How is't with you, my Lord?

Oth. Well my good Lady. Oh hardnes to dissemble!

How do you, Desdemona?
  Des. Well, my good Lord

  Oth. Giue me your hand.
This hand is moist, my Lady

Des. It hath felt no age, nor knowne no sorrow

  Oth. This argues fruitfulnesse, and liberall heart:
Hot, hot, and moyst. This hand of yours requires
A sequester from Liberty: Fasting, and Prayer,
Much Castigation, Exercise deuout,
For heere's a yong, and sweating Diuell heere
That commonly rebels: 'Tis a good hand,
A franke one

  Des. You may (indeed) say so:
For 'twas that hand that gaue away my heart

  Oth. A liberall hand. The hearts of old, gaue hands:
But our new Heraldry is hands, not hearts

  Des. I cannot speake of this:
Come, now your promise

  Oth. What promise, Chucke?
  Des. I haue sent to bid Cassio come speake with you

  Oth. I haue a salt and sorry Rhewme offends me:
Lend me thy Handkerchiefe

Des. Heere my Lord

Oth. That which I gaue you

Des. I haue it not about me

  Oth. Not?
  Des. No indeed, my Lord

  Oth. That's a fault: That Handkerchiefe
Did an aegyptian to my Mother giue:
She was a Charmer, and could almost read

The thoughts of people. She told her, while she kept it,
'T would make her Amiable, and subdue my Father
Intirely to her loue: But if she lost it,
Or made a Guift of it, my Fathers eye
Should hold her loathed, and his Spirits should hunt
After new Fancies. She dying, gaue it me,
And bid me (when my Fate would haue me Wiu'd)
To giue it her. I did so; and take heede on't,
Make it a Darling, like your precious eye:
To loose't, or giue't away, were such perdition,
As nothing else could match

  Des. Is't possible?
  Oth. 'Tis true: There's Magicke in the web of it:
A Sybill that had numbred in the world
The Sun to course, two hundred compasses,
In her Prophetticke furie sow'd the Worke:
The Wormes were hallowed, that did breede the Silke,
And it was dyde in Mummey, which the Skilfull
Conseru'd of Maidens hearts

  Des. Indeed? Is't true?
  Oth. Most veritable, therefore looke too't well

  Des. Then would to Heauen, that I had neuer seene't?
  Oth. Ha? wherefore?
  Des. Why do you speake so startingly, and rash?
  Oth. Is't lost? Is't gon? Speak, is't out o'th' way?
  Des. Blesse vs

  Oth. Say you?
  Des. It is not lost: but what and if it were?
  Oth. How?
  Des. I say it is not lost

Oth. Fetcht, let me see't

  Des. Why so I can: but I will not now:
This is a tricke to put me from my suite,
Pray you let Cassio be receiu'd againe

Oth. Fetch me the Handkerchiefe,
My minde mis-giues

Des. Come, come: you'l neuer meete a more sufficient
man

Oth. The Handkerchiefe

Des. A man that all his time
Hath founded his good Fortunes on your loue;
Shar'd dangers with you

Oth. The Handkerchiefe

Des. Insooth, you are too blame

Oth. Away.

Exit Othello.

Aemil. Is not this man iealious?
  Des. I neu'r saw this before.
Sure, there's some wonder in this Handkerchiefe,
I am most vnhappy in the losse of it.
Aemil. 'Tis not a yeare or two shewes vs a man:
They are all but Stomackes, and we all but Food,
They eate vs hungerly, and when they are full
They belch vs.
Enter Iago, and Cassio.

Looke you, Cassio and my Husband

  Iago. There is no other way: 'tis she must doo't:
And loe the happinesse: go, and importune her

  Des. How now (good Cassio) what's the newes with
you?
  Cassio. Madam, my former suite. I do beseech you,
That by your vertuous meanes, I may againe
Exist, and be a member of his loue,
Whom I, with all the Office of my heart
Intirely honour, I would not be delayd.

If my offence, be of such mortall kinde,
That nor my Seruice past, nor present Sorrowes,
Nor purpos'd merit in futurity,
Can ransome me into his loue againe,
But to know so, must be my benefit:
So shall I cloath me in a forc'd content,
And shut my selfe vp in some other course
To Fortunes Almes

  Des. Alas (thrice-gentle Cassio)
My Aduocation is not now in Tune;
My Lord, is not my Lord; nor should I know him,
Were he in Fauour, as in Humour alter'd.
So helpe me euery spirit sanctified,
As I haue spoken for you all my best,
And stood within the blanke of his displeasure
For my free speech. You must awhile be patient:
What I can do, I will: and more I will
Then for my selfe, I dare. Let that suffice you

  Iago. Is my Lord angry?
Aemil. He went hence but now:
And certainly in strange vnquietnesse

  Iago. Can he be angry? I haue seen the Cannon
When it hath blowne his Rankes into the Ayre,
And like the Diuell from his very Arme
Puff't his owne Brother: And is he angry?
Something of moment then: I will go meet him,
There's matter in't indeed, if he be angry.

Exit

  Des. I prythee do so. Something sure of State,
Either from Venice, or some vnhatch'd practise
Made demonstrable heere in Cyprus, to him,
Hath pudled his cleare Spirit: and in such cases,
Mens Natures wrangle with inferiour things,
Though great ones are their obiect. 'Tis euen so.
For let our finger ake, and it endues
Our other healthfull members, euen to a sense

Of paine. Nay, we must thinke men are not Gods,
Nor of them looke for such obseruancie
As fits the Bridall. Beshrew me much, aemilia,
I was (vnhandsome Warrior, as I am)
Arraigning his vnkindnesse with my soule:
But now I finde, I had suborn'd the Witnesse,
And he's Indited falsely.
Aemil. Pray heauen it bee
State matters, as you thinke, and no Conception,
Nor no Iealious Toy, concerning you

  Des. Alas the day, I neuer gaue him cause.
Aemil. But Iealious soules will not be answer'd so;
They are not euer iealious for the cause,
But iealious, for they're iealious. It is a Monster
Begot vpon it selfe, borne on it selfe

  Des. Heauen keepe the Monster from Othello's mind.
Aemil. Lady, Amen

  Des. I will go seeke him. Cassio, walke heere about:
If I doe finde him fit, Ile moue your suite,
And seeke to effect it to my vttermost.

Exit

  Cas. I humbly thanke your Ladyship.
Enter Bianca.

  Bian. 'Saue you (Friend Cassio.)
  Cassio. What make you from home?
How is't with you, my most faire Bianca?
Indeed (sweet Loue) I was comming to your house

  Bian. And I was going to your Lodging, Cassio.
What? keepe a weeke away? Seuen dayes, and Nights?
Eight score eight houres? And Louers absent howres
More tedious then the Diall, eight score times?
Oh weary reck'ning

  Cassio. Pardon me, Bianca:
I haue this while with leaden thoughts beene prest,

But I shall in a more continuate time
Strike off this score of absence. Sweet Bianca
Take me this worke out

  Bianca. Oh Cassio, whence came this?
This is some Token from a newer Friend,
To the felt-Absence: now I feele a Cause:
Is't come to this? Well, well

  Cassio. Go too, woman:
Throw your vilde gesses in the Diuels teeth,
From whence you haue them. You are iealious now,
That this is from some Mistris, some remembrance;
No, in good troth Bianca

  Bian. Why, who's is it?
  Cassio. I know not neither:
I found it in my Chamber,
I like the worke well; Ere it be demanded
(As like enough it will) I would haue it coppied:
Take it, and doo't, and leaue me for this time

  Bian. Leaue you? Wherefore?
  Cassio. I do attend heere on the Generall,
And thinke it no addition, nor my wish
To haue him see me woman'd

  Bian. Why, I pray you?
  Cassio. Not that I loue you not

  Bian. But that you do not loue me.
I pray you bring me on the way a little,
And say, if I shall see you soone at night?
  Cassio. 'Tis but a little way that I can bring you,
For I attend heere: But Ile see you soone

Bian. 'Tis very good: I must be circumstanc'd.

Exeunt. omnes.

Actus Quartus. Scena Prima.

Enter Othello, and Iago.

Iago. Will you thinke so?
Oth. Thinke so, Iago?
Iago. What, to kisse in priuate?
Oth. An vnauthoriz'd kisse?
Iago. Or to be naked with her Friend in bed,
An houre, or more, not meaning any harme?
Oth. Naked in bed (Iago) and not meane harme?
It is hypocrisie against the Diuell:
They that meane vertuously, and yet do so,
The Diuell their vertue tempts, and they tempt Heauen

Iago. If they do nothing, 'tis a Veniall slip:
But if I giue my wife a Handkerchiefe

Oth. What then?
Iago. Why then 'tis hers (my Lord) and being hers,
She may (I thinke) bestow't on any man

Oth. She is Protectresse of her honor too:
May she giue that?
Iago. Her honor is an Essence that's not seene,
They haue it very oft, that haue it not.
But for the Handkerchiefe

Othe. By heauen, I would most gladly haue forgot it:
Thou saidst (oh, it comes ore my memorie,
As doth the Rauen o're the infectious house:
Boading to all) he had my Handkerchiefe

Iago . I: what of that?
Othe. That's not so good now

Iag. What if I had said, I had seene him do you wrong?
Or heard him say (as Knaues be such abroad,
Who hauing by their owne importunate suit,
Or voluntary dotage of some Mistris,
Conuinced or supply'd them, cannot chuse
But they must blab.)
Oth. Hath he said any thing?

Iago. He hath (my Lord) but be you well assur'd,
No more then he'le vn-sweare

Oth. What hath he said?
Iago. Why, that he did: I know not what he did

Othe. What? What?
Iago. Lye

Oth. With her?
Iago. With her? On her: what you will

Othe. Lye with her? lye on her? We say lye on her, when they be-lye-her.
Lye with her: that's fullsome: Handkerchiefe: Confessions: Handkerchiefe.
To confesse, and be hang'd for his labour. First, to be hang'd, and then to
confesse: I tremble at it. Nature would not inuest her selfe in such
shadowing passion, without some Instruction. It is not words that shakes
me thus, (pish) Noses, Eares, and Lippes: is't possible. Confesse?
Handkerchiefe? O diuell.

Falls in a Traunce.

Iago. Worke on,
My Medicine workes. Thus credulous Fooles are caught,
And many worthy, and chast Dames euen thus,
(All guiltlesse) meete reproach: what hoa? My Lord?
My Lord, I say: Othello.
Enter Cassio.

How now Cassio?
Cas. What's the matter?
Iago. My Lord is falne into an Epilepsie,
This is his second Fit: he had one yesterday

Cas. Rub him about the Temples

Iago. The Lethargie must haue his quyet course:
If not, he foames at mouth: and by and by
Breakes out to sauage madnesse. Looke, he stirres:
Do you withdraw your selfe a little while,
He will recouer straight: when he is gone,
I would on great occasion, speake with you.

How is it Generall? Haue you not hurt your head?
  Othe. Dost thou mocke me?
  Iago. I mocke you not, by Heauen:
Would you would beare your Fortune like a Man

Othe. A Horned man's a Monster, and a Beast

  Iago. Ther's many a Beast then in a populous Citty,
And many a ciuill Monster

  Othe. Did he confesse it?
  Iago. Good Sir, be a man:
Thinke euery bearded fellow that's but yoak'd
May draw with you. There's Millions now aliue,
That nightly lye in those vnproper beds,
Which they dare sweare peculiar. Your case is better.
Oh, 'tis the spight of hell, the Fiends Arch-mock,
To lip a wanton in a secure Cowch;
And to suppose her chast. No, let me know,
And knowing what I am, I know what she shallbe

Oth. Oh, thou art wise: 'tis certaine

  Iago. Stand you a while apart,
Confine your selfe but in a patient List,
Whil'st you were heere, o're-whelmed with your griefe
(A passion most resulting such a man)
Cassio came hither: I shifted him away,
And layd good scuses vpon your Extasie,
Bad him anon returne: and heere speake with me,
The which he promis'd. Do but encaue your selfe,
And marke the Fleeres, the Gybes, and notable Scornes
That dwell in euery Region of his face.
For I will make him tell the Tale anew;
Where, how, how oft, how long ago, and when
He hath, and is againe to cope your wife.
I say, but marke his gesture: marry Patience,
Or I shall say y'are all in all in Spleene,
And nothing of a man

Othe. Do'st thou heare, Iago,
I will be found most cunning in my Patience:
But (do'st thou heare) most bloody

  Iago. That's not amisse,
But yet keepe time in all: will you withdraw?
Now will I question Cassio of Bianca,
A Huswife that by selling her desires
Buyes her selfe Bread, and Cloath. It is a Creature
That dotes on Cassio, (as 'tis the Strumpets plague
To be-guile many, and be be-guil'd by one)
He, when he heares of her, cannot restraine
From the excesse of Laughter. Heere he comes.
Enter Cassio.

As he shall smile, Othello shall go mad:
And his vnbookish Ielousie must conserue
Poore Cassio's smiles, gestures, and light behauiours
Quite in the wrong. How do you Lieutenant?
  Cas. The worser, that you giue me the addition,
Whose want euen killes me

  Iago. Ply Desdemona well, and you are sure on't:
Now, if this Suit lay in Bianca's dowre,
How quickely should you speed?
  Cas. Alas poore Caitiffe

Oth. Looke how he laughes already

Iago. I neuer knew woman loue man so

Cas. Alas poore Rogue, I thinke indeed she loues me

Oth. Now he denies it faintly: and laughes it out

  Iago. Do you heare Cassio?
  Oth. Now he importunes him
To tell it o're: go too, well said, well said

  Iago. She giues it out, that you shall marry her.
Do you intend it?
  Cas. Ha, ha, ha

Oth. Do ye triumph, Romaine? do you triumph?

Cas. I marry. What? A customer; prythee beare
Some Charitie to my wit, do not thinke it
So vnwholesome. Ha, ha, ha

Oth. So, so, so, so: they laugh, that winnes

Iago. Why the cry goes, that you marry her

Cas. Prythee say true

Iago. I am a very Villaine else

Oth. Haue you scoar'd me? Well

Cas. This is the Monkeys owne giuing out:
She is perswaded I will marry her
Out of her owne loue & flattery, not out of my promise

Oth. Iago becomes me: now he begins the story

Cassio. She was heere euen now: she haunts me in euery place. I was the
other day talking on the Seabanke with certaine Venetians, and thither
comes the Bauble, and falls me thus about my neck

Oth. Crying oh deere Cassio, as it were: his iesture imports
it

Cassio. So hangs, and lolls, and weepes vpon me:
So shakes, and pulls me. Ha, ha, ha

Oth. Now he tells how she pluckt him to my Chamber: oh, I see that nose
of yours, but not that dogge, I shall throw it to

Cassio. Well, I must leaue her companie

Iago. Before me: looke where she comes.
Enter Bianca.

Cas. 'Tis such another Fitchew: marry a perfum'd one? What do you
meane by this haunting of me? Bian. Let the diuell, and his dam haunt
you: what did you meane by that same Handkerchiefe, you gaue me euen
now? I was a fine Foole to take it: I must take out the worke? A likely

piece of worke, that you should finde it in your Chamber, and know not
who left it there. This is some Minxes token, & I must take out the worke?
There, giue it your Hobbey-horse, wheresoeuer you had it, Ile take out no
worke on't

  Cassio. How now, my sweete Bianca?
How now? How now?
  Othe. By Heauen, that should be my Handkerchiefe

  Bian. If you'le come to supper to night you may, if
you will not come when you are next prepar'd for.

Exit

Iago. After her: after her

Cas. I must, shee'l rayle in the streets else

  Iago. Will you sup there?
Cassio. Yes, I intend so

  Iago. Well, I may chance to see you: for I would very
faine speake with you

  Cas. Prythee come: will you?
Iago. Go too; say no more

Oth. How shall I murther him, Iago

  Iago. Did you perceiue how he laugh'd at his vice?
Oth. Oh, Iago

  Iago. And did you see the Handkerchiefe?
Oth. Was that mine?
Iago. Yours by this hand: and to see how he prizes
the foolish woman your wife: she gaue it him and, he
hath giu'n it his whore

  Oth. I would haue him nine yeeres a killing:
A fine woman, a faire woman, a sweete woman?
  Iago. Nay, you must forget that

Othello. I, let her rot and perish, and be damn'd to night, for she shall not liue. No, my heart is turn'd to stone: I strike it, and it hurts my hand. Oh, the world hath not a sweeter Creature: she might lye by an Emperours side, and command him Taskes

Iago. Nay, that's not your way

Othe. Hang her, I do but say what she is: so delicate with her Needle: an admirable Musitian. Oh she will sing the Sauagenesse out of a Beare: of so high and plenteous wit, and inuention? Iago. She's the worse for all this

Othe. Oh, a thousand, a thousand times:
And then of so gentle a condition?
  Iago. I too gentle

Othe. Nay that's certaine:
But yet the pitty of it, Iago: oh Iago, the pitty of it
Iago

Iago. If you are so fond ouer her iniquitie: giue her pattent to offend, for if it touch not you, it comes neere no body

Oth. I will chop her into Messes: Cuckold me?
Iago. Oh, 'tis foule in her

Oth. With mine Officer?
Iago. That's fouler

Othe. Get me some poyson, Iago, this night. Ile not expostulate with her: least her body and beautie vnprouide my mind againe: this night Iago

Iago. Do it not with poyson, strangle her in her bed,
Euen the bed she hath contaminated

Oth. Good, good:
The Iustice of it pleases: very good

Iago. And for Cassio, let me be his vndertaker:
You shall heare more by midnight.
Enter Lodouico, Desdemona, and Attendants.

Othe. Excellent good: What Trumpet is that same?
Iago. I warrant something from Venice,

'Tis Lodouico, this, comes from the Duke.
See, your wife's with him

Lodo. Saue you worthy Generall

Othe. With all my heart Sir

Lod. The Duke, and the Senators of Venice greet you

Othe. I kisse the Instrument of their pleasures

  Des. And what's the newes, good cozen Lodouico
  Iago. I am very glad to see you Signior:
Welcome to Cyprus

  Lod. I thanke you: how do's Lieutenant Cassio?
  Iago. Liues Sir,
  Des. Cozen, there's falne betweene him, & my Lord,
An vnkind breach: but you shall make all well

  Othe. Are you sure of that?
  Des. My Lord?
  Othe. This faile you not to do, as you will-
  Lod. He did not call: he's busie in the paper,
Is there deuision 'twixt my Lord, and Cassio?
  Des. A most vnhappy one: I would do much
T' attone, them, for the loue I beare to Cassio

Oth. Fire, and brimestone

Des. My Lord

  Oth. Are you wise?
  Des. What is he angrie?
  Lod. May be the Letter mou'd him.
For as I thinke, they do command him home,
Deputing Cassio in his Gouernment

Des. Trust me, I am glad on't

  Othe. Indeed?
  Des. My Lord?
  Othe. I am glad to see you mad

Des. Why, sweete Othello?
Othe. Diuell

Des. I haue not deseru'd this

Lod. My Lord, this would not be beleeu'd in Venice,
Though I should sweare I saw't. 'Tis very much,
Make her amends: she weepes

Othe. Oh diuell, diuell:
If that the Earth could teeme with womans teares,
Each drop she falls, would proue a Crocodile:
Out of my sight

Des. I will not stay to offend you

Lod. Truely obedient Lady:
I do beseech your Lordship call her backe

Othe. Mistris

Des. My Lord

Othe. What would you with her, Sir?
Lod. Who I, my Lord?
Othe. I, you did wish, that I would make her turne:
Sir, she can turne, and turne: and yet go on
And turne againe. And she can weepe, Sir, weepe.
And she's obedient: as you say obedient.
Very obedient: proceed you in your teares.
Concerning this Sir, (oh well-painted passion)
I am commanded home: get you away:
Ile send for you anon. Sir I obey the Mandate,
And will returne to Venice. Hence, auaunt:
Cassio shall haue my Place. And Sir, to night
I do entreat, that we may sup together.
You are welcome Sir to Cyprus.
Goates, and Monkeys.
Enter.

Lod. Is this the Noble Moore, whom our full Senate
Call all in all sufficient? Is this the Nature

Whom Passion could not shake? Whose solid vertue
The shot of Accident, nor dart of Chance
Could neither graze, nor pierce?
  Iago. He is much chang'd

  Lod. Are his wits safe? Is he not light of Braine?
  Iago. He's that he is: I may not breath my censure.
What he might be: if what he might, he is not,
I would to heauen he were

  Lod. What? Strike his wife?
  Iago. 'Faith that was not so well: yet would I knew
That stroke would proue the worst

  Lod. Is it his vse?
Or did the Letters, worke vpon his blood,
And new create his fault?
  Iago. Alas, alas:
It is not honestie in me to speake
What I haue seene, and knowne. You shall obserue him,
And his owne courses will denote him so,
That I may saue my speech: do but go after
And marke how he continues

Lod. I am sorry that I am deceiu'd in him.

Exeunt.

Scena Secunda.

Enter Othello and aemilia.

  Othe. You haue seene nothing then?
Aemil. Nor euer heard: nor euer did suspect

Othe. Yes, you haue seene Cassio, and she together

  Aemi. But then I saw no harme: and then I heard,
Each syllable that breath made vp betweene them

  Othe. What? Did they neuer whisper?
Aemil. Neuer my Lord

Othe. Nor send you out o'th' way?
Aemil. Neuer

  Othe. To fetch her Fan, her Gloues, her Mask, nor nothing?
Aemil. Neuer my Lord

  Othe. That's strange.
Aemil. I durst (my Lord) to wager, she is honest:
Lay downe my Soule at stake: If you thinke other,
Remoue your thought. It doth abuse your bosome:
If any wretch haue put this in your head,
Let Heauen requit it with the Serpents curse,
For if she be not honest, chaste, and true,
There's no man happy. The purest of their Wiues
Is foule as Slander

Othe. Bid her come hither: go.

Exit aemilia.

She saies enough: yet she's a simple Baud
That cannot say as much. This is a subtile Whore:
A Closset Locke and Key of Villanous Secrets,
And yet she'le kneele, and pray: I haue seene her do't.
Enter Desdemona, and aemilia.

  Des. My Lord, what is your will?
Othe. Pray you Chucke come hither

  Des. What is your pleasure?
Oth. Let me see your eyes: looke in my face

  Des. What horrible Fancie's this?
Othe. Some of your Function Mistris:
Leaue Procreants alone, and shut the doore:
Cough, or cry hem; if any body come:
Your Mystery, your Mystery: May dispatch.

Exit aemi.

  Des. Vpon my knee, what doth your speech import?
I vnderstand a Fury in your words

Othe. Why? What art thou?
  Des. Your wife my Lord: your true and loyall wife

Othello. Come sweare it: damne thy selfe, least being like one of Heauen,
the diuells themselues should feare to ceaze thee. Therefore be double
damn'd: sweare thou art honest

Des. Heauen doth truely know it

Othe. Heauen truely knowes, that thou art false as hell

  Des. To whom my Lord?
With whom? How am I false?
  Othe. Ah Desdemon, away, away, away

  Des. Alas the heauy day: why do you weepe?
Am I the motiue of these teares my Lord?
If happely you my Father do suspect,
An Instrument of this your calling backe,
Lay not your blame on me: if you haue lost him,
I haue lost him too

  Othe. Had it pleas'd Heauen,
To try me with Affliction, had they rain'd
All kind of Sores, and Shames on my bare-head:
Steep'd me in pouertie to the very lippes.
Giuen to Captiuitie, me, and my vtmost hopes,
I should haue found in some place of my Soule
A drop of patience. But alas, to make me
The fixed Figure for the time of Scorne,
To point his slow, and mouing finger at.
Yet could I beare that too, well, very well:
But there where I haue garnerd vp my heart,
Where either I must liue, or beare no life,
The Fountaine from the which my currant runnes,
Or else dries vp: to be discarded thence,
Or keepe it as a Cesterne, for foule Toades
To knot and gender in. Turne thy complexion there:
Patience, thou young and Rose-lip'd Cherubin,
I heere looke grim as hell

Des. I hope my Noble Lord esteemes me honest

Othe. Oh I, as Sommer Flyes are in the Shambles,
That quicken euen with blowing. Oh thou weed:
Who art so louely faire, and smell'st so sweete,
That the Sense akes at thee,
Would thou had'st neuer bin borne

Des. Alas, what ignorant sin haue I committed?
Othe. Was this faire Paper? This most goodly Booke
Made to write Whore vpon? What commited,
Committed? Oh, thou publicke Commoner,
I should make very Forges of my cheekes,
That would to Cynders burne vp Modestie,
Did I but speake thy deedes. What commited?
Heauen stoppes the Nose at it, and the Moone winks:
The baudy winde that kisses all it meetes,
Is hush'd within the hollow Myne of Earth
And will not hear't. What commited?
Des. By Heauen you do me wrong

Othe. Are not you a Strumpet?
Des. No, as I am a Christian.
If to preserue this vessell for my Lord,
From any other foule vnlawfull touch
Be not to be a Strumpet, I am none

Othe. What, not a Whore?
Des. No, as I shall be sau'd

Othe. Is't possible?
Des. Oh Heauen forgiue vs

Othe. I cry you mercy then.
I tooke you for that cunning Whore of Venice,
That married with Othello. You Mistris,
Enter aemilia.

That haue the office opposite to Saint Peter,
And keepes the gate of hell. You, you: I you.
We haue done our course: there's money for your paines:
I pray you turne the key, and keepe our counsaile.
Enter.

Aemil. Alas, what do's this Gentleman conceiue?
How do you Madam? how do you my good Lady?
  Des. Faith, halfe a sleepe

  Aemi. Good Madam,
What's the matter with my Lord?
  Des. With who?
Aemil. Why, with my Lord, Madam?
  Des. Who is thy Lord?
Aemil. He that is yours, sweet Lady

  Des. I haue none: do not talke to me, aemilia,
I cannot weepe: nor answeres haue I none,
But what should go by water. Prythee to night,
Lay on my bed my wedding sheetes, remember,
And call thy husband hither.
Aemil. Heere's a change indeed.
Enter.

  Des. 'Tis meete I should be vs'd so: very meete.
How haue I bin behau'd, that he might sticke
The small'st opinion on my least misvse?
Enter Iago, and aemilia.

  Iago. What is your pleasure Madam?
How is't with you?
  Des. I cannot tell: those that do teach yong Babes
Do it with gentle meanes, and easie taskes.
He might haue chid me so; for in good faith
I am a Child to chiding

  Iago. What is the matter Lady?
Aemil. Alas (Iago) my Lord hath so bewhor'd her,
Throwne such dispight, and heauy termes vpon her
That true hearts cannot beare it

  Des. Am I that name, Iago?
  Iago. What name, (faire Lady?)
  Des. Such as she said my Lord did say I was.
Aemil. He call'd her whore: a Begger in his drinke:
Could not haue laid such termes vpon his Callet

Iago. Why did he so?
Des. I do not know: I am sure I am none such

Iago. Do not weepe, do not weepe: alas the day.
Aemil. Hath she forsooke so many Noble Matches?
Her Father? And her Country? And her Friends?
To be call'd Whore? Would it not make one weepe?
Des. It is my wretched Fortune

Iago. Beshrew him for't:
How comes this Tricke vpon him?
Des. Nay, Heauen doth know

Aemi. I will be hang'd, if some eternall Villaine,
Some busie and insinuating Rogue,
Some cogging, cozening Slaue, to get some Office,
Haue not deuis'd this Slander: I will be hang'd else

Iago. Fie, there is no such man: it is impossible

Des. If any such there be, Heauen pardon him.
Aemil. A halter pardon him:
And hell gnaw his bones.
Why should he call her Whore?
Who keepes her companie?
What Place? What Time?
What Forme? What liklyhood?
The Moore's abus'd by some most villanous Knaue,
Some base notorious Knaue, some scuruy Fellow.
Oh Heauens, that such companions thou'd'st vnfold,
And put in euery honest hand a whip
To lash the Rascalls naked through the world,
Euen from the East to th' West

Iago. Speake within doore.
Aemil. Oh fie vpon them: some such Squire he was
That turn'd your wit, the seamy-side without,
And made you to suspect me with the Moore

Iago. You are a Foole: go too

Des. Alas Iago,
What shall I do to win my Lord againe?
Good Friend, go to him: for by this light of Heauen,
I know not how I lost him. Heere I kneele:
If ere my will did trespasse 'gainst his Loue,
Either in discourse of thought, or actuall deed,
Or that mine Eyes, mine Eares, or any Sence
Delighted them: or any other Forme.
Or that I do not yet, and euer did,
And euer will, (though he do shake me off
To beggerly diuorcement) Loue him deerely,
Comfort forsweare me. Vnkindnesse may do much,
And his vnkindnesse may defeat my life,
But neuer taynt my Loue. I cannot say Whore,
It do's abhorre me now I speake the word,
To do the Act, that might the addition earne,
Not the worlds Masse of vanitie could make me

Iago. I pray you be content: 'tis but his humour:
The businesse of the State do's him offence

Des. If 'twere no other

Iago. It is but so, I warrant,
Hearke how these Instruments summon to supper:
The Messengers of Venice staies the meate,
Go in, and weepe not: all things shall be well.

Exeunt. Desdemona and aemilia.

Enter Rodorigo.

How now Rodorigo?
  Rod. I do not finde
That thou deal'st iustly with me

Iago. What in the contrarie? Rodori. Euery day thou dafts me with some
deuise Iago, and rather, as it seemes to me now, keep'st from me all
conueniencie, then suppliest me with the least aduantage of hope: I will
indeed no longer endure it. Nor am I yet perswaded to put vp in peace,
what already I haue foolishly suffred

Iago. Will you heare me Rodorigo?

Rodori. I haue heard too much: and your words and
Performances are no kin together

Iago. You charge me most vniustly

Rodo. With naught but truth: I haue wasted my selfe out of my meanes.
The Iewels you haue had from me to deliuer Desdemona, would halfe
haue corrupted a Votarist. You haue told me she hath receiu'd them, and
return'd me expectations and comforts of sodaine respect, and
acquaintance, but I finde none

Iago. Well, go too: very well

Rod. Very well, go too: I cannot go too, (man) nor 'tis not very well. Nay I
think it is scuruy: and begin to finde my selfe fopt in it

Iago. Very well

Rodor. I tell you, 'tis not very well: I will make my selfe knowne to
Desdemona. If she will returne me my Iewels, I will giue ouer my Suit, and
repent my vnlawfull solicitation. If not, assure your selfe, I will seeke
satisfaction of you

Iago. You haue said now

Rodo. I: and said nothing but what I protest intendment of doing

Iago. Why, now I see there's mettle in thee: and euen from this instant do
build on thee a better opinion then euer before: giue me thy hand
Rodorigo. Thou hast taken against me a most iust exception: but yet I
protest I haue dealt most directly in thy Affaire

Rod. It hath not appeer'd

Iago. I grant indeed it hath not appeer'd: and your suspition is not without
wit and iudgement. But Rodorigo, if thou hast that in thee indeed, which I
haue greater reason to beleeue now then euer (I meane purpose, Courage,
and Valour) this night shew it. If thou the next night following enioy not
Desdemona, take me from this world with Treacherie, and deuise Engines
for my life

Rod. Well: what is it? Is it within, reason and compasse?

Iago. Sir, there is especiall Commission come from
Venice to depute Cassio in Othello's place

Rod. Is that true? Why then Othello and Desdemona
returne againe to Venice

Iago. Oh no: he goes into Mauritania and taketh away with him the faire
Desdemona, vnlesse his abode be lingred heere by some accident.
Wherein none can be so determinate, as the remouing of Cassio

Rod. How do you meane remouing him?

Iago. Why, by making him vncapable of Othello's
place: knocking out his braines

Rod. And that you would haue me to do

Iago. I: if you dare do your selfe a profit, and a right. He sups to night with
a Harlotry: and thither will I go to him. He knowes not yet of his
Honourable Fortune, if you will watch his going thence (which I will
fashion to fall out betweene twelue and one) you may take him at your
pleasure. I will be neere to second your Attempt, and he shall fall
betweene vs. Come, stand not amaz'd at it, but go along with me: I will
shew you such a necessitie in his death, that you shall thinke your selfe
bound to put it on him. It is now high supper time: and the night growes
to wast. About it

Rod. I will heare further reason for this

Iago. And you shalbe satisfi'd.

Exeunt.

Scena Tertia.

Enter Othello, Lodouico, Desdemona, aemilia, and Atendants.

Lod. I do beseech you Sir, trouble your selfe no further

Oth. Oh pardon me: 'twill do me good to walke

Lodoui. Madam, good night: I humbly thanke your
Ladyship

Des. Your Honour is most welcome

Oth. Will you walke Sir? Oh Desdemona

Des. My Lord

Othello. Get you to bed on th' instant, I will be return'd
forthwith: dismisse your Attendant there: look't
be done.
Enter.

Des. I will my Lord

Aem. How goes it now? He lookes gentler then he did

Des. He saies he will returne incontinent,
And hath commanded me to go to bed,
And bid me to dismisse you

Aemi. Dismisse me?
Des. It was his bidding: therefore good aemilia,
Giue me my nightly wearing, and adieu.
We must not now displease him.
Aemil. I, would you had neuer seene him

Des. So would not I: my loue doth so approue him,
That euen his stubbornesse, his checks, his frownes,
(Prythee vn-pin me) haue grace and fauour

Aemi. I haue laid those Sheetes you bad me on the bed

Des. All's one: good Father, how foolish are our minds?
If I do die before, prythee shrow'd me
In one of these same Sheetes.
Aemil. Come, come: you talke

Des. My Mother had a Maid call'd Barbarie,
She was in loue: and he she lou'd prou'd mad,
And did forsake her. She had a Song of Willough,
An old thing 'twas: but it express'd her Fortune,

And she dy'd singing it. That Song to night,
Will not go from my mind: I haue much to do,
But to go hang my head all at one side
And sing it like poore Barbarie: prythee dispatch

  Aemi. Shall I go fetch your Night-gowne?
  Des. No, vn-pin me here,
This Lodouico is a proper man.
Aemil. A very handsome man

Des. He speakes well. Aemil. I know a Lady in Venice would haue walk'd
barefoot to Palestine for a touch of his nether lip

  Des. The poore Soule sat singing, by a Sicamour tree.
Sing all a greene Willough:
Her hand on her bosome her head on her knee,
Sing Willough, Willough, Willough.
The fresh Streames ran by her, and murmur'd her moanes
Sing Willough, &c.
Her salt teares fell from her, and softned the stones,
Sing Willough, &c. (Lay by these)
Willough, Willough. (Prythee high thee: he'le come anon)
Sing all a greene Willough must be my Garland.
Let no body blame him, his scorne I approue.
(Nay that's not next. Harke, who is't that knocks?
Aemil. It's the wind

  Des. I call'd my Loue false Loue: but what said he then?
Sing Willough, &c.
If I court mo women, you'le couch with mo men.
So get thee gone, good night: mine eyes do itch:
Doth that boade weeping?
Aemil. 'Tis neyther heere, nor there

  Des. I haue heard it said so. O these Men, these men!
Do'st thou in conscience thinke (tell me aemilia)
That there be women do abuse their husbands
In such grosse kinde?
Aemil. There be some such, no question

Des. Would'st thou do such a deed for all the world?

Aemil. Why, would not you?

 Des. No, by this Heauenly light.

Aemil. Nor I neither, by this Heauenly light:
I might doo't as well i'th' darke

 Des. Would'st thou do such a deed for al the world?

Aemil. The world's a huge thing:
It is a great price, for a small vice

Des. Introth, I thinke thou would'st not. Aemil. Introth I thinke I should, and vndoo't when I had done. Marry, I would not doe such a thing for a ioynt Ring, nor for measures of Lawne, nor for Gownes, Petticoats, nor Caps, nor any petty exhibition. But for all the whole world: why, who would not make her husband a Cuckold, to make him a Monarch? I should venture Purgatory for't

Des. Beshrew me, if I would do such a wrong For the whole world. Aemil. Why, the wrong is but a wrong i'th' world; and hauing the world for your labour, 'tis a wrong in your owne world, and you might quickly make it right

 Des. I do not thinke there is any such woman.

Aemil. Yes, a dozen: and as many to'th' vantage, as
would store the world they plaid for.
But I do thinke it is their Husbands faults
If Wiues do fall: (Say, that they slacke their duties,
And powre our Treasures into forraigne laps;
Or else breake out in peeuish Iealousies,
Throwing restraint vpon vs: Or say they strike vs,
Or scant our former hauing in despight)
Why we haue galles: and though we haue some Grace,
Yet haue we some Reuenge. Let Husbands know,
Their wiues haue sense like them: They see, and smell,
And haue their Palats both for sweet, and sowre,
As Husbands haue. What is it that they do,
When they change vs for others? Is it Sport?
I thinke it is: and doth Affection breed it?
I thinke it doth. Is't Frailty that thus erres?
It is so too. And haue not we Affections?
Desires for Sport? and Frailty, as men haue?

Then let them vse vs well: else let them know,
The illes we do, their illes instruct vs so

   Des. Good night, good night:
Heauen me such vses send,
Not to picke bad, from bad; but by bad, mend.

Exeunt.

Actus Quintus. Scena Prima.

Enter Iago, and Rodorigo.

   Iago. Heere, stand behinde this Barke,
Straight will he come:
Weare thy good Rapier bare, and put it home:
Quicke, quicke, feare nothing; Ile be at thy Elbow,
It makes vs, or it marres vs, thinke on that,
And fixe most firme thy Resolution

Rod. Be neere at hand, I may miscarry in't

Iago. Heere, at thy hand: Be bold, & take thy stand

   Rod. I haue no great deuotion to the deed,
And yet he hath giuen me satisfying Reasons:
'Tis but a man gone. Forth my Sword: he dies

   Iago. I haue rub'd this yong Quat almost to the sense,
And he growes angry. Now, whether he kill Cassio,
Or Cassio him, or each do kill the other,
Euery way makes my gaine. Liue Rodorigo,
He calles me to a restitution large
Of Gold, and Iewels, that I bob'd from him,
As Guifts to Desdemona.
It must not be: If Cassio do remaine,
He hath a dayly beauty in his life,
That makes me vgly: and besides, the Moore
May vnfold me to him: there stand I in much perill:
No, he must dye. But so, I heard him comming.
Enter Cassio.

Rod. I know his gate, 'tis he: Villaine thou dyest

  Cas. That thrust had beene mine enemy indeed,
But that my Coate is better then thou know'st:
I will make proofe of thine

Rod. Oh, I am slaine

  Cassio. I am maym'd for euer:
Helpe hoa: Murther, murther.
Enter Othello.

Oth. The voyce of Cassio. Iago keepes his word

Rod. O Villaine that I am

Oth. It is euen so

Cas. Oh helpe hoa: Light, a Surgeon

  Oth. 'Tis he: O braue Iago, honest, and iust,
That hast such Noble sense of thy Friends wrong,
Thou teachest me. Minion, your deere lyes dead,
And your vnblest Fate highes: Strumpet I come:
For of my heart, those Charmes thine Eyes, are blotted.
Thy Bed lust-stain'd, shall with Lusts blood bee spotted.

Exit Othello.

Enter Lodouico and Gratiano.

  Cas. What hoa? no Watch? No passage?
Murther, Murther

Gra. 'Tis some mischance, the voyce is very direfull

Cas. Oh helpe

Lodo. Hearke

Rod. Oh wretched Villaine

Lod. Two or three groane. 'Tis heauy night;
These may be counterfeits: Let's think't vnsafe
To come into the cry, without more helpe

Rod. Nobody come: then shall I bleed to death.
Enter Iago.

Lod. Hearke

Gra. Here's one comes in his shirt, with Light, and
Weapons

Iago. Who's there?
Who's noyse is this that cries on murther?
Lodo. We do not know

Iago. Do not you heare a cry?
Cas. Heere, heere: for heauen sake helpe me

Iago. What's the matter?
Gra. This is Othello's Ancient, as I take it

Lodo. The same indeede, a very valiant Fellow

Iago. What are you heere, that cry so greeuously?
Cas. Iago? Oh I am spoyl'd, vndone by Villaines:
Giue me some helpe

Iago. O mee, Lieutenant!
What Villaines haue done this?
Cas. I thinke that one of them is heereabout.
And cannot make away

Iago. Oh treacherous Villaines:
What are you there? Come in, and giue some helpe

Rod. O helpe me there

Cassio. That's one of them

Iago. Oh murd'rous Slaue! O Villaine!
Rod. O damn'd Iago! O inhumane Dogge!
Iago. Kill men i'th' darke?

Where be these bloody Theeues?
How silent is this Towne? Hoa, murther, murther.
What may you be? Are you of good, or euill?
  Lod. As you shall proue vs, praise vs

  Iago. Signior Lodouico?
Lod. He Sir

Iago. I cry you mercy: here's Cassio hurt by Villaines

  Gra. Cassio?
Iago. How is't Brother?
Cas. My Legge is cut in two

  Iago. Marry heauen forbid:
Light Gentlemen, Ile binde it with my shirt.
Enter Bianca.

  Bian. What is the matter hoa? Who is't that cry'd?
Iago. Who is't that cry'd?
  Bian. Oh my deere Cassio,
My sweet Cassio: Oh Cassio, Cassio, Cassio

  Iago. O notable Strumpet. Cassio, may you suspect
Who they should be, that haue thus mangled you?
  Cas. No

  Gra. I am sorry to finde you thus;
I haue beene to seeke you

  Iago. Lend me a Garter. So: - Oh for a Chaire
To beare him easily hence

Bian. Alas he faints. Oh Cassio, Cassio, Cassio

  Iago. Gentlemen all, I do suspect this Trash
To be a party in this Iniurie.
Patience awhile, good Cassio. Come, come;
Lend me a Light: know we this face, or no?
Alas my Friend, and my deere Countryman
Rodorigo? No: Yes sure: Yes, 'tis Rodorigo

Gra. What, of Venice?

Iago. Euen he Sir: Did you know him?

Gra. Know him? I

Iago. Signior Gratiano? I cry your gentle pardon:
These bloody accidents must excuse my Manners,
That so neglected you

Gra. I am glad to see you

Iago. How do you Cassio? Oh, a Chaire, a Chaire

Gra. Rodorigo?

Iago. He, he, 'tis he:
Oh that's well said, the Chaire.
Some good man beare him carefully from hence,
Ile fetch the Generall's Surgeon. For you Mistris,
Saue you your labour. He that lies slaine heere (Cassio)
Was my deere friend. What malice was between you

Cas. None in the world: nor do I know the man?

Iago. What? looke you pale? Oh beare him o'th' Ayre.
Stay you good Gentlemen. Looke you pale, Mistris?
Do you perceiue the gastnesse of her eye?
Nay, if you stare, we shall heare more anon.
Behold her well: I pray you looke vpon her:
Do you see Gentlemen? Nay, guiltinesse will speake
Though tongues were out of vse.

Aemil. Alas, what is the matter?
What is the matter, Husband?

Iago. Cassio hath heere bin set on in the darke
By Rodorigo, and Fellowes that are scap'd:
He's almost slaine, and Rodorigo quite dead.

Aemil. Alas good Gentleman: alas good Cassio

Iago. This is the fruits of whoring. Prythe aemilia,
Go know of Cassio where he supt to night.
What, do you shake at that?

Bian. He supt at my house, but I therefore shake not

Iago. O did he so? I charge you go with me.

Aemil. Oh fie vpon thee Strumpet

Bian. I am no Strumpet, but of life as honest,
As you that thus abuse me.
Aemil. As I? Fie vpon thee

Iago. Kinde Gentlemen:
Let's go see poore Cassio drest.
Come Mistris, you must tel's another Tale.
aemilia, run you to the Cittadell,
And tell my Lord and Lady, what hath happ'd:
Will you go on afore? This is the night
That either makes me, or foredoes me quight.

Exeunt.

Scoena Secunda.

Enter Othello, and Desdemona in her bed.

Oth. It is the Cause, it is the Cause (my Soule)
Let me not name it to you, you chaste Starres,
It is the Cause. Yet Ile not shed her blood,
Nor scarre that whiter skin of hers, then Snow,
And smooth as Monumentall Alablaster:
Yet she must dye, else shee'l betray more men:
Put out the Light, and then put out the Light:
If I quench thee, thou flaming Minister,
I can againe thy former light restore,
Should I repent me. But once put out thy Light,
Thou cunning'st Patterne of excelling Nature,
I know not where is that Promethaean heate
That can thy Light re-Lume.
When I haue pluck'd thy Rose,
I cannot giue it vitall growth againe,
It needs must wither. Ile smell thee on the Tree.
Oh Balmy breath, that dost almost perswade
Iustice to breake her Sword. One more, one more:
Be thus when thou art dead, and I will kill thee,
And loue thee after. One more, and that's the last.
So sweet, was ne're so fatall. I must weepe,
But they are cruell Teares: This sorrow's heauenly,
It strikes, where it doth loue. She wakes

Des. Who's there? Othello?
Othel. I Desdemona

 Des. Will you come to bed, my Lord?
 Oth. Haue you pray'd to night, Desdemon?
 Des. I my Lord

 Oth. If you bethinke your selfe of any Crime
Vnreconcil'd as yet to Heauen, and Grace,
Solicite for it straight

 Des. Alacke, my Lord,
What may you meane by that?
 Oth. Well, do it, and be breefe, I will walke by:
I would not kill thy vnprepared Spirit,
No, Heauens fore-fend) I would not kill thy Soule

 Des. Talke you of killing?
 Oth. I, I do

Des. Then Heauen haue mercy on mee

Oth. Amen, with all my heart

Des. If you say, I hope you will not kill me

Oth. Humh

 Des. And yet I feare you: for you're fatall then
When your eyes rowle so.
Why I should feare, I know not,
Since guiltinesse I know not: But yet I feele I feare

Oth. Thinke on thy sinnes

Des. They are Loues I beare to you

Oth. I, and for that thou dy'st

 Des. That death's vnnaturall, that kils for louing.
Alas, why gnaw you so your nether-lip?
Some bloody passion shakes your very Frame:

These are portents: but yet I hope, I hope,
They do not point on me

Oth. Peace, and be still

   Des. I will so: What's the matter?
   Oth. That Handkerchiefe
Which I so lou'd, and gaue thee, thou gau'st to Cassio

   Des. No by my Life, and Soule: send for the man,
And aske him

   Oth. Sweet Soule, take heed, take heed of Periury,
Thou art on thy death-bed

Des. I, but not yet to dye

   Oth. Presently.
Therefore confesse thee freely of thy sinne:
For to deny each Article with Oath,
Cannot remoue, nor choake the strong Conception
That I do grone withall. Thou art to dye

Des. O Heauen haue mercy on me

Oth. I say, Amen

   Des. And haue you mercy too. I neuer did
Offend you in my life: neuer lou'd Cassio,
But with such generall warrantie of Heauen,
As I might loue. I neuer gaue him Token

   Oth. By Heauen I saw my Handkerchiefe in's hand.
O periur'd woman, thou do'st stone my heart,
And makes me call, what I intend to do,
A Murther, which I thought a Sacrifice.
I saw the Handkerchiefe

   Des. He found it then:
I neuer gaue it him: Send, for him hither:
Let him confesse a truth

Oth. He hath confest

Des. What, my Lord?
Oth. That he hath vs'd thee

Des. How? vnlawfully?
Oth. I

Des. He will not say so

Oth. No: his mouth is stopp'd:
Honest Iago hath 'tane order for't

Des. Oh, my feare interprets. What is he dead?
Oth. Had all his haires bin liues, my great Reuenge
Had stomacke for them all

Des. Alas, he is betray'd, and I vndone

Oth. Out Strumpet: weep'st thou for him to my face?
Des. O banish me, my Lord, but kill me not

Oth. Downe Strumpet

Des. Kill me to morrow, let me liue to night

Oth. Nay, if you striue

Des. But halfe an houre

Oth. Being done, there is no pawse

Des. But while I say one prayer

Oth. It is too late.

Smothers her.

aemilia at the doore.

Aemil. My Lord, my Lord? What hoa?
My Lord, my Lord

Oth. What noise is this? Not dead? not yet quite dead?
I that am cruell, am yet mercifull,

I would not haue thee linger in thy paine?
So, so.
Aemil. within. What hoa? my Lord, my Lord?
  Oth. Who's there?
Aemil. Oh good my Lord, I would speake a word
with you

  Oth. Yes: 'Tis aemilia: by and by. Shee's dead.
'Tis like she comes to speake of Cassio's death:
The noise was high. Hah, no more moouing?
Still as the Graue. Shall she come in? Wer't good?
I thinke she stirres againe. No, what's best to do?
If she come in, shee'l sure speake to my wife:
My wife, my wife: what wife? I haue no wife.
Oh insupportable! Oh heauy houre!
Me thinkes, it should be now a huge Eclipse
Of Sunne, and Moone; and that th' affrighted Globe
Did yawne at Alteration.
Aemil. I do beseech you
That I may speake with you. Oh good my Lord

  Oth. I had forgot thee: oh come in aemilia.
Soft, by and by, let me the Curtaines draw.
Where art thou? What's the matter with thee now?
Enter aemilia.

Aemil. Oh my good Lord, yonders foule Murthers done

  Oth. What? now?
Aemil. But now, my Lord

  Oth. It is the very error of the Moone,
She comes more neerer Earth then she was wont,
And makes men mad.
Aemil. Cassio, my Lord, hath kill'd
A young Venetian, call'd Rodorigo

  Oth. Rodorigo kill'd? and Cassio kill'd?
Aemil. No, Cassio is not kill'd

  Oth. Not Cassio kill'd? Then Murther's out of tune,
And sweet Reuenge growes harsh

Des. O falsely, falsely murder'd.
Aemil. Alas! what cry is that?
  Oth. That? What?
Aemil. Out, and alas, that was my Ladies voice.
Helpe, helpe hoa, helpe. Oh Ladie speake againe,
Sweet Desdemona, oh sweet Mistris, speake

  Des. A guiltlesse death, I dye.
Aemil. Oh who hath done this deed?
  Des. No body: I my selfe, farewell:
Commend me to my kinde Lord: oh farewell

  Oth. Why, how should she be murdred?
Aemil. Alas: who knowes?
  Oth. You heare her say her selfe, it was not I.
Aemil. She said so: I must needs report the truth

  Oth. She's like a Liar gone to burning hell,
'Twas I that kill'd her.
Aemil. Oh the more Angell she, and you the blacker
Diuell

  Oth. She turn'd to folly: and she was a whore.
Aemil. Thou do'st bely her, and thou art a diuell

  Oth. She was false as water.
Aemil. Thou art rash as fire, to say
That she was false. Oh she was heauenly true

  Oth. Cassio did top her: Ask thy husband else.
O, I were damn'd beneath all depth in hell:
But that I did proceed vpon iust grounds
To this extremity. Thy Husband knew it all.
Aemil. My Husband?
  Oth. Thy Husband.
Aemil. That she was false to Wedlocke?
  Oth. I, with Cassio: had she bin true,
If Heauen would make me such another world,
Of one entyre and perfect Chrysolite,
I'ld not haue sold her for it.
Aemil. My Husband?

Oth. I, 'twas he that told me on her first,
An honest man he is, and hates the slime
That stickes on filthy deeds.
Aemil. My Husband?
  Oth. What needs this itterance, Woman?
I say, thy Husband.
Aemil. Oh Mistris,
Villany hath made mockes with loue:
My Husband say she was false?
  Oth. He, Woman;
I say thy Husband: Do'st vnderstand the word?
My Friend, thy Husband; honest, honest Iago.
Aemil. If he say so, may his pernicious Soule
Rot halfe a graine a day: he lyes to'th' heart,
She was too fond of her most filthy Bargaine

  Oth. Hah?
Aemil. Do thy worst:
This deede of thine is no more worthy Heauen,
Then thou was't worthy her

  Oth. Peace, you were best.
Aemil. Thou hast not halfe that powre to do me harm,
As I haue to be hurt. Oh Gull, oh dolt,
As ignorant as durt: thou hast done a deed
(I care not for thy Sword) Ile make thee known,
Though I lost twenty liues. Helpe, helpe, hoa, helpe:
The Moore hath kill'd my Mistris. Murther, murther.
Enter Montano, Gratiano, and Iago.

  Mon. What is the matter? How now Generall?
Aemil. Oh, are you come, Iago: you haue done well,
That men must lay their Murthers on your necke

  Gra. What is the matter?
Aemil. Disproue this Villaine, if thou bee'st a man:
He sayes, thou told'st him that his wife was false:
I know thou did'st not: thou'rt not such a Villain.
Speake, for my heart is full

Iago. I told him what I thought,
And told no more
Then what he found himselfe was apt, and true.
Aemil. But did you euer tell him,
She was false?
Iago. I did.
Aemil. You told a Lye an odious damned Lye:
Vpon my Soule, a Lye; a wicked Lye.
Shee false with Cassio?
Did you say with Cassio?
Iago. With Cassio, Mistris?
Go too, charme your tongue

Emil. I will not charme my Tongue;
I am bound to speake,
My Mistris heere lyes murthered in her bed

All. Oh Heauens, forefend

Emil. And your reports haue set the Murder on

Othello. Nay stare not Masters,
It is true indeede

Gra. 'Tis a strange Truth

Mont. O monstrous Acte

Emil. Villany, villany, villany:
I thinke vpon't, I thinke: I smel't: O Villany:
I thought so then: Ile kill my selfe for greefe.
O villany! villany!
Iago. What, are you mad?
I charge you get you home

Emil. Good Gentlemen, let me haue leaue to speake:
'Tis proper I obey him; but not now:
Perchance Iago, I will ne're go home

Oth. Oh, oh, oh

Emil. Nay, lay thee downe, and roare:
For thou hast kill'd the sweetest innocent,
That ere did lift vp eye

Oth. Oh she was fowle!
I scarse did know you Vnkle, there lies your Neece,
Whose breath (indeed) these hands haue newly stopp'd:
I know this acte shewes horrible and grim

Gra. Poore Desdemon:
I am glad thy Father's dead,
Thy Match was mortall to him: and pure greefe
Shore his old thred in twaine. Did he liue now,
This sight would make him do a desperate turne:
Yea, curse his better Angell from his side,
And fall to Reprobance

Oth. 'Tis pittifull: but yet Iago knowes
That she with Cassio, hath the Act of shame
A thousand times committed. Cassio confest it,
And she did gratifie his amorous workes
With that Recognizance and pledge of Loue
Which I first gaue her: I saw it in his hand:
It was a Handkerchiefe, an Antique Token
My Father gaue my Mother

Emil. Oh Heauen! oh heauenly Powres!
Iago. Come, hold your peace

Emil. 'Twill out, 'twill out. I peace?
No, I will speake as liberall as the North;
Let Heauen, and Men, and Diuels, let them all,
All, all, crie shame against me, yet Ile speake

Iago. Be wise, and get you home

Emil. I will not

Gra. Fye, your Sword vpon a Woman

Emil. Oh thou dull Moore,
That Handkerchiefe thou speak'st of

I found by Fortune, and did giue my Husband:
For often, with a solemne earnestnesse,
(More then indeed belong'd to such a Trifle)
He begg'd of me, to steale't

Iago. Villanous Whore

  Emil. She giue it Cassio? No, alas I found it,
And I did giu't my Husband

Iago. Filth, thou lyest

  Emil. By Heauen I do not, I do not Gentlemen:
Oh murd'rous Coxcombe, what should such a Foole
Do with so good a wife?
  Oth. Are there no stones in Heauen,
But what serues for the Thunder?
Precious Villaine

  Gra. The woman falles:
Sure he hath kill'd his Wife

Emil. I, I: oh lay me by my Mistris side

Gra. Hee's gone, but his wife's kill'd

  Mon. 'Tis a notorious Villain: take you this weapon
Which I haue recouer'd from the Moore:
Come guard the doore without, let him not passe,
But kill him rather. Ile after that same villaine,
For 'tis a damned Slaue.
Enter.

  Oth. I am not valiant neither:
But euery Punie whipster gets my Sword.
But why should Honor out-liue Honesty?
Let it go all.
Aemil. What did thy Song boad Lady?
Hearke, canst thou heare me? I will play the Swan,
And dye in Musicke: Willough, Willough, Willough.
Moore, she was chaste: She lou'd thee, cruell Moore,

So come my Soule to blisse, as I speake true:
So speaking as I thinke, alas, I dye

  Oth. I haue another weapon in this Chamber,
It was a Sword of Spaine, the Ice brookes temper:
Oh heere it is: Vnkle I must come forth

  Gra. If thou attempt it, it will cost thee deere;
Thou hast no weapon, and perforce must suffer

  Oth. Looke in vpon me then, and speake with me,
Or naked as I am I will assault thee

  Gra. What is the matter?
  Othel. Behold, I haue a weapon:
A better neuer did it selfe sustaine
Vpon a Soldiers Thigh. I haue seene the day,
That with this little Arme, and this good Sword,
I haue made my way through more impediments
Then twenty times your stop. But (oh vaine boast)
Who can controll his Fate? 'Tis not so now.
Be not affraid, though you do see me weapon'd:
Heere is my iournies end, heere is my butt
And verie Sea-marke of my vtmost Saile.
Do you go backe dismaid? 'Tis a lost feare:
Man but a Rush against Othello's brest,
And he retires. Where should Othello go?
Now: how dost thou looke now? Oh ill-Starr'd wench,
Pale as thy Smocke: when we shall meete at compt,
This looke of thine will hurle my Soule from Heauen,
And Fiends will snatch at it. Cold, cold, my Girle?
Euen like thy Chastity. O cursed, cursed Slaue!
Whip me ye Diuels,
From the possession of this Heauenly sight:
Blow me about in windes, roast me in Sulphure,
Wash me in steepe-downe gulfes of Liquid fire.
Oh Desdemon! dead Desdemon: dead. Oh, oh!
Enter Lodouico, Cassio, Montano, and Iago, with Officers.

  Lod. Where is this rash, and most vnfortunate man?
  Oth. That's he that was Othello: heere I am

Lod. Where is that Viper?
Bring the Villaine forth

   Oth. I look down towards his feet; but that's a Fable,
If that thou bee'st a Diuell, I cannot kill thee

Lod. Wrench his Sword from him

Iago. I bleed Sir, but not kill'd

   Othel. I am not sorry neither, Il'd haue thee liue:
For in my sense, 'tis happinesse to die

   Lod. Oh thou Othello, that was once so good,
Falne in the practise of a cursed Slaue,
What shall be saide to thee

   Oth. Why any thing:
An honourable Murderer, if you will:
For nought I did in hate, but all in Honour

   Lod. This wretch hath part confest his Villany:
Did you and he consent in Cassio's death

Oth. I

Cas. Deere Generall, I neuer gaue you cause

   Oth. I do beleeue it, and I aske your pardon:
Will you, I pray, demand that demy-Diuell,
Why he hath thus ensnar'd my Soule and Body

   Iag. Demand me nothing: what you know, you know:
From this time forth, I neuer will speake word

   Lod. What? not to pray?
   Gra. Torments will ope your lips

Oth. Well, thou dost best

   Lod. Sir,
You shall vnderstand what hath befalne,
(Which, as I thinke, you know not) heere is a Letter

Found in the pocket of the slaine Rodorigo,
And heere another, the one of them imports
The death of Cassio, to be vndertooke
By Rodorigo

  Oth. O Villaine!
  Cassio. Most Heathenish, and most grosse

  Lod. Now, heere's another discontented paper
Found in his pocket too: and this it seemes
Rodorigo meant t'haue sent this damned villaine:
But that (belike) Iago in the interim
Came in, and satisfi'd him

  Oth. Oh thou pernitious Caitiffe;
How came you (Cassio) by that Handkerchiefe
That was my wiues?
  Cassio. I found it in my Chamber:
And he himselfe confest it but euen now,
That there he dropt it for a speciall purpose,
Which wrought to his desire

  Othel. O Foole, foole, foole!
  Cassio. There is besides, in Rodorigo's Letter,
How he vpbraides Iago, that he made him
Braue me vpon the Watch: whereon it came
That I was cast: and euen but now he spake
(After long seeming dead) Iago hurt him,
Iago set him on

  Lod. You must forsake this roome, and go with vs:
Your Power, and your Command is taken off,
And Cassio rules in Cyprus. For this Slaue,
If there be any cunning Crueltie,
That can torment him much, and hold him long,
It shall be his. You shall close Prisoner rest,
Till that the Nature of your fault be knowne
To the Venetian State. Come, bring away

  Oth. Soft you; a word or two before you goe:
I haue done the State some seruice, and they know't:

No more of that. I pray you in your Letters,
When you shall these vnluckie deeds relate,
Speake of me, as I am. Nothing extenuate,
Nor set downe ought in malice.
Then must you speake,
Of one that lou'd not wisely, but too well:
Of one, not easily Iealious, but being wrought,
Perplexed in the extreame: Of one, whose hand
(Like the base Iudean) threw a Pearle away
Richer then all his Tribe: Of one, whose subdu'd Eyes,
Albeit vn-vsed to the melting moode,
Drops teares as fast as the Arabian Trees
Their Medicinable gumme. Set you downe this:
And say besides, that in Aleppo once,
Where a malignant, and a Turbond-Turke
Beate a Venetian, and traduc'd the State,
I tooke by th' throat the circumcised Dogge,
And smoate him, thus

Lod. Oh bloody period

Gra. All that is spoke, is marr'd

  Oth. I kist thee, ere I kill'd thee: No way but this,
Killing my selfe, to dye vpon a kisse.

Dyes

  Cas. This did I feare, but thought he had no weapon:
For he was great of heart

  Lod. Oh Sparton Dogge:
More fell then Anguish, Hunger, or the Sea:
Looke on the Tragicke Loading of this bed:
This is thy worke:
The Obiect poysons Sight,
Let it be hid. Gratiano, keepe the house,
And seize vpon the Fortunes of the Moore,
For they succeede on you. To you, Lord Gouernor,
Remaines the Censure of this hellish villaine:
The Time, the Place, the Torture, oh inforce it:

My selfe will straight aboord, and to the State,
This heauie Act, with heauie heart relate.

Exeunt.

FINIS.

The Names of the Actors.

Othello, the Moore.
Brabantio, Father to Desdemona.
Cassio, an Honourable Lieutenant.
Iago, a Villaine.
Rodorigo, a gull'd Gentleman.
Duke of Venice.
Senators.
Montano, Gouernour of Cyprus.
Gentlemen of Cyprus.
Lodouico, and Gratiano, two Noble Venetians.
Saylors.
Clowne.
Desdemona, Wife to Othello.
Aemilia, Wife to Iago.
Bianca, a Curtezan.

THE TRAGEDIE OF Othello, the Moore of Venice.

Printed in Great Britain
by Amazon.co.uk, Ltd.,
Marston Gate.